THE DOORS OF THE CHURCH ARE CLOSED

Dana Carson, D.Min., Ph.D.

PRESS

DEDICATION

This book is dedicated to my family, and in particular, my lovely wife, who is my primary editor. If it was not for her support, I would not have been able to complete this book. Thank you, Rachelle, for your vote of confidence in my preaching, teaching, and writing. I also want thank my children who are the breath that I breathe. I hope that this writing will forever give you direction in your spiritual life and journey and to understand the heart and call of your father long after I have departed. Thank you for sharing me with the world! Also I would like to render an acknowledgment to my deceased parents, former sharecroppers, who provided for me a tremendous platform to succeed because of their love and nurture. I would also like to thank God for my spiritual fathers — Apostle E. W. Wilcots and Apostle R. D. Henton. I would like to thank Bishop Charles Blake Jr. for his continual faith and encouraging words. I would like to thank my best friend Tony Wilcots for the gift of friendship. There are two former professors of mine that I want to give special acknowledgement to for their encouragement in writing this book — Dr. Trevor Grizzle and Dr. Brad Young. I would like to thank my staff for their continual support and my chief of staff, Norman Campbell, for being a faithful ministry partner and friend, and his wife Lynette for sharing him with me and the church staff. But most of all, I would like to thank God for giving me the insight and inspiration to write to the glory of His Kingdom.

The Doors of the Church are Closed Endorsements

> In *The Doors of the Church are Closed,* Dr. Carson artfully distills and blends the best insights of scholarly inquiry and the practical and pastoral implications of the Kingdom of God for the contemporary church and society. This book is not an echo of popular clichéd jargon, but a fresh clarion call to biblical Kingdom living.
>
> **Dr. Trevor Grizzle**
> **Professor of New Testament**
> **Oral Roberts University**

FROM DR. SHANNON CORMIER:

This book will, without a doubt, go down in the annals of religious history as one of the most revolutionary writings of the Christian Church. The levels of illumination found on the pages of this book will inevitably position Dr. Carson as a voice of reformation for a 21st century church. In an era in which the altar has been compromised and repentance is non-existent, his writing calls for the church to consider its ways and repent! Every Bible scholar, seminary student, pastor, and layperson will be challenged at the core of their Christianity after reading this phenomenal work!

Shannon Cormier, Ph.D.
Executive Vice President, Texas Black Expo

FROM DR. BRAD YOUNG:

Dr. Carson's new book will be a blessing to everyone studying the message of Jesus concerning the Kingdom and the urgent need for reconciliation. His teachings will stimulate debate and bring healing.

Dr. Brad Young
Professor of Biblical Literature
Oral Roberts University

FROM BISHOP HAWKINS:

Once again Dr. Dana Carson has proven to be on the cutting edge with the powerful truths of the Kingdom of God. *The Doors of the Church are Closed* brings revelation as well as empowers and liberates the believer to experience a relationship with God in a new and living way. Thank you Dr. Carson for a life-changing word! The Kingdom of God is truly at hand.

Bishop Felton Hawkins, Senior Pastor
Full Gospel Kingdom Church
Newport News, VA

Preface

"The Doors of the Church are Closed" originated from a series of prophetic messages that I preached describing where the body of Christ is on the time line of God. What do we mean when we say that the doors of the church are now closed? One major clue is referenced in the Book of Revelation, third chapter, verses 14 - 21, where Jesus is knocking on the doors of the Church of Laodicea. Jesus is standing at the closed doors of His church, imploring those on the other side to open the door so that He can fellowship with them. The people on the other side of that door are so spiritually deluded that they do not even recognize that they are miserable, poor, blind, naked and wretched.

This imagery precisely defines the times and the season in which the Church is currently operating. Many in today's church, believing themselves to be safe from all alarm, are being led by Satan on a path to eternal separation from God. They have, knowingly or unknowingly, rejected Jesus and are not a part of His Kingdom. The central theme in contemporary churches is a 'spiritualized humanism' that feeds into the people's self-centeredness and massages their sinful nature. Christ can only be fully formed in us through the Word of God and if the Word of God is not being preached

in its entirety and placed contextually into 21ˢᵗ century secu-
larism, there will be no transformation in the lives of those
listening to empty messages that have style but no substance.
We exist in an age where sermons have a form of godliness
but deny its power and purpose, as warned in the opening
text of 2 Timothy, chapter three.

The most critical issue revealed in the Revelation text
is the depth of deception because those who are deceived
actually see themselves as devout, committed worshippers
of God. They are members of the church who no longer
have the sensitivity or desire to listen to the governmental
voice of God. Positionally and functionally, they appear to
be members of Christ's church... the only problem is that
they have abandoned Christ!

I propose that there is a horrific dynamic occurring in
today's church, whereby culture, social tradition, and the
individual have supplanted the King and His will. Sound
doctrine and the Word of God have lost their primacy in
favor of a self-centered "gospel" that exalts the creature
over the Creator. We seek God's hand and not His face; He
has become another means to secular ends grounded in our
carnality. Have you visited such a church lately?

TABLE OF CONTENTS

A FAULTY FOUNDATION

Before we delve into how and why this is occurring in our churches, we must lay the proper foundation. In any living organism, a solid foundation is critical to sound and healthy growth. The growth of the human body is contingent upon a solid foundation of health built upon dietary issues, exercise, and stress management. It is next to impossible to produce healthy growth without a solid foundation. Did you know that many sicknesses are due to our initial eating habits? It is argued in some schools of thought that diseases once thought to be based upon genetics, or nature, are really due to environment, or nurture. In essence, the diseases that we are plagued with are due to our ancestors' poor eating habits, lack of exercise, and mismanagement of stress. We have been groomed and socialized to eat what they ate and mimic the same unhealthy behavioral norms. We are products of our environments — a generation of 'mini me's'.

You can observe the same cyclical patterns forming a foundational dynamic in marriage. A marriage's health is also predicated upon its foundation. It is very difficult, in fact it's virtually impossible, to experience a healthy marital relationship if the foundation is faulty. For example, a marriage will be unhealthy and an uphill battle if its foundation was birthed out of sexual pressure/fornication, esteem issues, pregnancy (especially shotgun weddings), social/family pressure, the fear of aging, ignorance or unfamiliarity with each other, unrealistic expectations, or an affair. When these are the issues that motivate us to enter into a marital relationship, divorce is inevitable, either mentally, physically, or both. You cannot build growing organisms, organizations, and structures based on a faulty foundation. In the area of behavioral sciences, we are trained not simply to examine or focus upon the presentation of the problems or the effects of the problem, we are trained to investigate the problem so that we can get to the root issue and cause. Every problem has a root cause.

This is the correct approach to problems and issues if we have a vested interest in finding a solution. When Jesus came to minister in our world, it was said of Him by His predecessor, John the Baptist, that when He came He would put the axe at the root. (Matthew 3:10) Humanity's sin condition could only be solved at the root or the foundation. The Mosaic Law, guiding the morality of God's people until Christ's arrival, dealt with the effects of sin, which meant that sin had to constantly be atoned for. But Christ addressed sin at its foundation, our sin nature, because we are all born in sin and shaped in iniquity. Christ had to tear down the entire construct of our existence; He condemned the old structure represented by the Law because of its faulty foundational issues. He created a new foundation in order for humanity to experience solid and healthy growth. Thank God for a new foundation! Since you can only become as healthy as your foundation will allow, we must have a good foundation. Foundation is everything! (1 Corinthians 3:11)

That's one of the reasons people say that you can tell a tree by the fruit it bears. People will also tell you that an apple does not fall far from its tree. When you are counseling your children, sound parental advice about making a selection for marital relationships always should include advising them to do a little family background investigation. That's because you can tell a lot about how people are going to be by their family paradigm. Foundations are extremely important.

Before employers hire employees, they perform a background check to see what your work 'foundation' is, and if they find out that you've only held jobs for two or three months at a time, then they may tell you, "We're sorry, we don't want to hire you because you have a faulty foundation."

Before you can get into institutions of higher learning, they are going to examine your educational history to make sure that you have the proper foundation to be able to handle their curriculum. You can't even get into a post-graduate program without them knowing your GRE, GMAT, MCAT or LSAT scores - or whatever their examination requirements are. If you're going into a doctoral program, a PhD program, they will want to know that you have a sufficient background in research, a solid graduate school foundation, and have successfully mastered multiple languages.

The point is that without a solid foundation you cannot expect solid or healthy growth, barring a miracle. Foundations give us a reasonable basis for predictability, which brings us to the issue of the Christian church in America and its impact abroad.

An objective look at today's church will find that it is irrelevant regarding spiritual matters due to a faulty foundation. Its foundation is based upon socioeconomics, class, culture, and race. That assessment alone makes it almost impossible to yield a healthy, growing spiritual institution. The contemporary church is a sociological phenomenon, masquerading as an organism that belongs to God, when it is actually an organism that reflects the social, cultural and traditional norms of society. The church that you see is not the church that Jesus designed and purposed nor does it reflect the church's development under the leadership of the early church fathers. In its present form and function, devoid of God's power and purpose...it is a perversion.

According to well-documented research, we are losing over 3,000 - 4,000 American Christian churches annually, which means church doors are closing, never to open again. That same research indicates that we are starting about 1200 churches annually, some say as high as 1800 per year.[1] These statistics translate into the loss of about 1200 to 2200 Christian churches a year. Why aren't people coming to church? I thought the doors of the church were open. Some may ask, "What about the mega church movement; isn't it growing?" Well, research suggests that 97% of Christian churches in America *did not win one person to Christ* in the last year.[2] Statistics clearly indicate how infrequently evangelism takes place; some studies suggest that it takes 85 Christians to make one convert over a year's time. Most churches that are referred to as mega churches are not growing based on their conversion of sinners or biological growth but based on transfer growth. People are simply leaving other churches! These mega churches are drying up some of the 'founded in 1947' churches that have not changed their worship services since 1947. People are leaving the corner "Mom and Pop" church for the giant Wal-Mart church down the road. People are leaving these churches because they are sick and tired of the same unfulfilling experience, the numbers in their home churches are dwindling, and they now want to be part of something that seems progressive. These Christians are willing to go to the other extreme, even if it means the compromise of doctrine.

Another startling fact - the former members of dying churches are choosing one of three options when they leave those churches. One option, as I call it, is the "the Feel Good Church." After all, those persons think, "I'm a believer but I'm down, my church died and I need to feel good." Recent research found that Roman Catholicism lost more adherents than any other in U.S. religious group.[3] The second option is Islam or other religious experiences. Christians are converting to Islam at a higher rate then any other religious persuasion. I believe that this reality is because of the turbulent history of American Christianity. People are possibly sick and tired of the very obvious division that exists in the Christian church and are looking for something that is more religious in nature verses that which is clearly social in nature. The third option is independent spirituality, or non-organized spiritualism. This, in my estimation, is the natural development of secular humanism and intellectualism. These two schools of thought have provided the confidence in self and the priority of self to create a foundation for people to engage in subjective spirituality. Thus, their spirituality emulates from situational ethics and selfish endeavors without clear definition or purpose.

Why is the American church not successful in its mission? Because its foundation is not conducive for evangelism and discipleship. How can this be when John Naisbitt, in his book *Megatrends (1982)*, predicted that the phenomenon of a high-tech, low-touch society would create a desire for people to frequent spaces that have a high-touch because they miss people's touch and intimacy? How is it that this lack isn't creating what should be the church's finest hour, with the unsaved flocking through the church's opened doors on a weekly basis? How is it that instead we are in our most troubled hour?

A growing and healthy church...the first century church gives us the best model for what the church of Jesus Christ should look, think, and act like. Without question, the early church was an explosive movement.

And with many other words he testified and exhorted them, saying, "Be saved from this perverse generation." Then those who gladly received His Word were baptized; and that day about three thousand souls were added to them. And they continued steadfastly in the apostles' doctrine and fellowship, in the breaking of bread, and in prayers. Then fear came upon every soul, and many wonders and signs were done through the apostles. Now all who believed were together, and had all things in common, and sold their possessions and goods, and divided them among all, as anyone had need. So continuing daily with one accord in the temple, and breaking bread from house to house, they ate their food with gladness and simplicity of heart, praising God and having favor with all the people. And the Lord added to the church daily those who were being saved. (Acts 2:40-47)

In stark contrast to the contemporary church, the early Church experienced three major things:

1. It preached repentance, separation from this perverse generation, and salvation
2. Upon hearing the message, *the people* asked what they must do [to be saved]
3. The Lord added thousands to the church *daily*

Occurrences of these phenomena are rare, if not non-existent, in America. The Bible teaches us that only God can grow a church and that unless the Lord builds the house, people that labor, labor in vain. How true that is! So, if the church in America is on the decline, why isn't God's demonstrated growth principle working for us? (Mark 4:26-29) Alternatively, what has happened between the Church's initial explosive movement and now to render these principles extinct on the ecclesiastical landscape?

THE CHURCH: THE GREAT DECEPTION

Obviously, the 1st century church preached an extremely compelling message! Their message was convicting and controversial because they preached, taught, and demonstrated what Jesus preached, taught, and demonstrated — the Kingdom of God. The proclamation of the Kingdom of God was central to Christ's message – it is recorded numerous times in each of the synoptic gospels (Matthew, Mark, Luke and John). In Luke 4:43, Jesus said He must preach the Kingdom of God.

The topic of the Kingdom of God was paramount to John the Baptist, Jesus, and His disciples. Curiously, however, we do not hear much about the Kingdom of God in our churches today. Over 2000 years later, the concept of the Kingdom of God is at worst, unknown and at best, misunderstood. Most people think that the Kingdom of God is where we go when we die. In addition, since Matthew was a devout Jew who refused to use the name of God, people think there is a difference between the Kingdom of heaven (Matthew's reference) and the Kingdom of God – but there is no such difference! The church does NOT equal the Kingdom of God. Likewise, church membership is not synonymous with Kingdom of God citizenship.

There is a valid reason for this misunderstanding. The Word of God covers a wide span of history, so underlying every element of text is a context, culture, and cause. When engaging in the art of interpreting biblical text, referred to as hermeneutics or exegesis by theologians, one must determine if there is *value* in that particular passage in our current context or whether its application is simply restricted and relegated to the historical set of facts and circumstances in which it was penned. Therefore, the essence of any biblical text cannot be fully understood unless you understand the context in which God's Scripture was authored. In order to truly comprehend the differing concepts of the Kingdom of God and the church, this aspect must be pain-stakingly considered. Another equally significant aspect to consider in evaluating the role, responsibility, and reckoning of Christ's contemporary church is the concept of dispensationalism.

A *dispensation* is a particular period of time marked by specific parameters that are relevant to a given era. Everything is governed by the dispensation in which it originates: people, revelations, events, evolution, understanding, yes, the entire world. I refer to dispensations as 'times and seasons'. The Bible teaches about divine providence and omniscience, which implies that God is in complete control and is bringing all things together to manifest His will; everything is headed in one specific direction. Since there will be one climatic closure, the Bible includes prophecies and other pieces of information that will enable us to properly align ourselves with God's divine timetable for humanity. God has done unique things during specific times that give these events an inherent marking or dating, and He will continue to do so. The biblical information we are given is to be used to assist us in interpreting the times and seasons so that we can be like the sons of Issachar and know what to do.

Further examination of dispensationalism teaches that Biblical history is composed of a number of successive economies or administrations called dispensations, each of which emphasizes the continuity of the Old Testament covenants God made with His chosen people through His chosen leaders, Abraham, Moses, and King David. In the context of Christianity, dispensationalism is an interpretive, narrative framework for understanding the overall flow of the Bible. Dispensationalism is frequently contrasted with an opposing interpretation of the Bible called super-sessionism, also referred to as "covenant theology." In simple terms, super-sessionism teaches that the Christian church has been established for the salvation of the Jews first, then also the Gentiles, and that there is one people of God joined in unity through Jesus Christ.

By contrast, dispensationalism teaches that the Christian church is a part of God's progressive relationship with the Jews. In the first century, the Gospel began to spread to the Gentiles instead of the Jews because of their conscious rejection of Christ. However, God's continued favor for the Jews will be revealed after the dispensation known as the church age, when the Jews will be restored to their own land and will claim Jesus as their Messiah. Dispensationalists believe in Jewish restoration.

Now let me help you with these two concepts and explain what makes differentiating them so important when I assert that "The doors of the church are closed." Super-sessionism suggests that all Jews and Gentiles came together in Christ, meaning God no longer has any specific use for any Jews who don't believe in Jesus as the Christ. This would mean that after Christ came and gave the Jewish nation an opportunity to embrace Him and they did not, God was totally finished with them. Why? Because they ignored the Way, the Truth, and the Life and no man can come to God except through Christ (John 14:6). Dispensationalists, however, believe that Christ came to the Jew first and then to the Gentile (Romans 1:16-17), but when the panoramic flow of Scripture is considered, God is not through with Israel. Even though God engrafted non-Jews into the covenant He established for Jews, He still has a special purpose for Israel. In the book of Romans, Paul dedicates a special section of his writing to explain this to believers in Rome (Romans 11).

When we read this Pauline epistle, it is clear that God has a continuing purpose for the Jewish people based upon the prophecies in the Hebrew Scriptures (Old Testament) and the New Testament. On the prophetic clock of God, which is theologically based on events that have occurred or are prophesied to occur, the most recent of the great prophecies has occurred in our lifetime: the prophecy of Ezekiel 36, 37, and 38. In these chapters, God promised the prophet Ezekiel that there would come a time after the Diaspora [i.e., the dispersion of the Jews to all four corners of the earth] when He would miraculously bring Israel together and once again they would occupy their own nation. In 1948, against the odds, Israel did indeed become an independent nation. While there have been enemies that have surrounded Israel, they have not been able to defeat them. The year 1948 legitimized one of the most important prophecies in the Bible - and has brought us up to contemporary times on the prophetic clock of God. Now the next major prophetic event that has to take place is that the gospel of the Kingdom be preached as a sign, and then the world shall come to a culmination (Matthew 24:14). So when we consider the prophetic clock of God, the events of church history, today's headlines, and the growing interest in the Kingdom of God, these all suggests that we are entering the next theological dispensation. I strongly believe that we have entered into the seventh or the last dispensation prior to the Rapture, or snatching away, of the Bride of Christ, His true church, the remnant that preaches the Kingdom!

God works in dispensations and dispensationalists generally agree on the following Seven Dispensations of Theology:

- ➤ Dispensation of innocence - prior to Adam's fall;
- ➤ Dispensation of conscience - Adam to Noah;
- ➤ Dispensation of government - Noah to Abraham;
- ➤ Dispensation of patriarchal rule - Abraham to Moses;
- ➤ Dispensation of the Mosaic Law - Moses to Christ;
- ➤ Dispensation of grace - the current church age: and
- ➤ Dispensation of Millennial Kingdom – eschatological reign of Jesus Christ

Each dispensation delineated a change in the way in which God dealt with mankind with respect to the questions of sin and responsibility and often presents a unique challenge for humanity. C.I. Scofield has said that each of the dispensations may be regarded as a new test of the natural man and each ends in judgment, marking his utter failure in each and every dispensation. We are currently living in the dispensation of grace. But the dispensation of grace or the church age has also experienced its own sub-dispensations, which we will discuss later. Ignorance and misunderstanding, therefore, abound not only because of the failures of mankind but also due to the prophetic clock of God – it has been destined to occur that way. Then, just as now, He has destined you to walk fully in the knowledge and understanding of His Kingdom.

The passage of time and persistent ignorance of the distinction between the church and the Kingdom of God have seeded strange beliefs into the paradigm we understand as Christianity. The best standard to test the authenticity of the church today, however, is the 1st century church. That the early church fathers actually served Jesus and Jesus' plan to develop the church was revealed in a conversation with Peter.

> *And with many other words he testified and exhorted them, saying, "Be saved from this perverse generation." Then those who gladly received His Word were baptized; and that day about three thousand souls were added to them. And they continued steadfastly in the apostles' doctrine and fellowship, in the breaking of bread, and in prayers. Then fear came upon every soul, and many wonders and signs were done through the apostles. Now all who believed were together, and had all things in common, and sold their possessions and goods, and divided them among all, as anyone had need. So continuing daily with one accord in the temple, and breaking bread from house to house, they ate their food with gladness and simplicity of heart, praising God and having favor with all the people. And the Lord added to the church daily those who were being saved. (Acts 2:40-47)*

One problem we have is people choose to join or not join the church, in contrast to the early church where believers were added to the Lord or the Lord added to the church. Unfortunately, people choose church simply based upon a consumers mentality. People are choosing churches based upon their branding, marketing position, and competitive edge. People are joining the church of the highest bidder! When we closely examine the Acts 2:47 text, the scripture reads that the Lord added to the church daily, those who were being saved. People received eternal life and then they received their responsibility of service. Do you get that? First, they were saved and then they were dispatched for service. All believers are reconciled back to God with an assignment. Then God places each of us as spiritual beings in the earth realm for the purpose of giving birth to what He actually deposited in us before the beginning of time. If you are saved and don't serve, something is wrong with your salvation. Today, though, it is not uncommon to have 'church folks' struggle just to make it to church then essentially *refuse* to serve because of the busy-ness of their lives. Every one that gives their heart to Christ is supposed to be working in the church, performing a particular area of ministry service.

The believers in Acts did not merely 'join the church'; that was something that God did. He added them to the church, those who were being saved. Notice that there is a difference between being saved and adding to the church. Some older translations even omit the word 'church'. The word 'added' is a significant and insightful word. In the Greek, the word *prostithemi* means to place near, to add to, to hand over, or to include in a society. So, when it says the Lord added to the church, it refers to Him handing converts over, which implies His relationship and sovereignty is primary, and adding them to the church.

But He was not adding numbers to an idle, stagnant membership, but to an aggressive people who came to be known for turning the world upside down. We must recognize that the 1st century church was on a Kingdom mission and sensitive to the voice of God; God laid the foundation of the church by using them. Thus scripture states "except the Lord build a house they that labor do so in vain". We've come to learn through the researched principles of natural church development and church health that there is really no such thing as church growth. Mankind cannot 'grow' a church. While there is nothing inherently wrong with contemporary churches utilizing tactics to make themselves attractive, the church cannot rely upon slick marketing and business practices to grow ministries. The church must rely upon the empowerment of the Holy Spirit to be a witness for Christ as the compelling element that drives people, first, to the altar, and ultimately to service in the church. The only thing a church can do is create a healthy environment and remove environmental resistance. The Lord has to grow the church. The success of the apostolic, or 1st century, church was not its marketing department or its children's ministry, but the strength of the people's witness of the resurrection. And God led converts to the church daily.

Unfortunately, many of us have, at some point in time in our Christian church experience, heard the church invitation: "The doors of the church are open, will there be one? You can come by letter, baptism, or Christian experience." This statement has misled millions of people, because the Bible doesn't teach that the church has doors for a new believer to enter. Of course, there are those that argue that the reference to the opening of the doors of the church is actually a reference to the Kingdom. It is important to restate that there is a distinction between the church and the Kingdom of God because they are not synonymous. Since they are not the same, we cannot say we're simply dealing with semantics. The difference between entering the Kingdom and being added to the church vs. opening the doors of the church and joining makes all the difference in the world! What is really happening at the altar?

The two most important institutions to God are the church and the Kingdom; unfortunately, there is controversy surrounding them both. While most people are aware of the reality and concept of the church, they are fairly ignorant regarding the Kingdom. To compound matters, those who are familiar with the concept of church interpret it through the prisms of race and class. The church has become a sociological phenomenon in our contemporary society that is divided based on the issues of race, class, sex, and denominationalism. It is difficult to imagine or even conceive of a kingdom, and certainly not God's Kingdom, divided along those lines. It is precisely because of these distracting influences that the church and the Kingdom cannot be interpreted as synonymous in nomenclature.

The church is clearly not the Kingdom of God and the Kingdom of God is clearly not the church. Rather, both of these institutions serve together in a symbiotic relationship. The two, while being separate and inextricably bound throughout their history, have held erroneous views about each other, such that extreme confusion exists among the people of God. Most contemporary Christians see themselves as members of the church but not citizens of the Kingdom. Here's my emergency newsflash: if you have only joined the church and have not been born again, you do not have a relationship with the Lord Jesus Christ! You are simply wasting your time "playing church" without the benefit of eternal life. The Bible says that except a man is born again, he cannot see the Kingdom, nor can he enter, the Kingdom. (John 3:5, 6) The Bible says that except you become like little children, you will not enter the Kingdom (Matthew 18:3).

The church only has value if she leads others into the Kingdom. Roman Catholic scholar John Fuellenbach, in his 1995 book, *The Kingdom of God: The Message of Jesus Today*, expresses that the church is *not* the Kingdom of God upon the earth. He states that the term or phrase "Kingdom of God" is more comprehensive term than"church".[4] Fuellenbach and many other scholars from different theological camps are in agreement that the Kingdom of God cannot be defined through the limited scope of church.

Although the church and the Kingdom are not synonymous, we must not minimize the importance of the church when it is properly functioning as the instrument of the Kingdom. Simply stated, the church is the custodian or the servant of the Kingdom, thus, if the church is not serving the Kingdom, it is not the church that Jesus Christ built. Jesus gave the church the keys to the Kingdom, and if the church is simply opening its own doors, it has become an idolatrous self-serving institution that has totally confused and aborted its spiritual assignment. The church has prostituted the influence of God by not directing people into His Kingdom, but rather directing them unto itself in an egotistical orgy of me-ism and materialism. It is a classic bait and switch, but with eternal consequences.

One of the general definitions of the Kingdom of God set forth by New Testament scholar George Ladd, in his 1959 book, *The Gospel of the Kingdom,* is that the Kingdom of God is the divine redemptive rule manifested in Christ and the realm in which the blessings of His divine rule may be experienced. It is the reign of God, not simply in the hearts of men, but also in their minds. Ladd points to at least five differences between the church and the Kingdom: [5]

➢ The church is not the kingdom
➢ The kingdom creates the church
➢ The church witnesses to the kingdom
➢ The church is the instrument of the kingdom
➢ The church is the custodian of the kingdom

He also examines the following passage in which Jesus said to Peter:

> *"And I say also unto thee, That thou art Peter, and upon this rock I will build my church; and the gates of hell shall not prevail against it. And I will give unto thee the keys of the kingdom of heaven..." (Matthew 16:18, 19)*

In this passage, Jesus is moving in thought from the 'church' to the Kingdom. He is not referring to the church as the Kingdom nor the Kingdom as the church. The Kingdom of heaven (God) predated the church and then the *Kingdom created the church*. The church is the creation of the Kingdom. It is a model, a copy, an imitation, and a small reflection of the real thing. The role of the church is to tell people about the Kingdom, and then be used by the Kingdom. Lastly, the church holds the keys to the Kingdom, allowing entrance and potentially denying access. For Christians in today's dispensation, the shallow distinction that they make between these two concepts is in their understanding of who will directly influence their spirituality, spiritual longevity and, ultimately, their eternal destination.

Christ, His Church, and Its Identity

The church has been a significant factor in Christendom since the 1st century. Though the church is primarily a New Testament phenomenon, it is present in principle and practice in the Old Testament. As we begin to take a closer look at what the Bible teaches about the church, much is revealed through a linguistic analysis of the words that are primarily used for church in God's word.

- *Qahal* means "a special assembly", or "to assemble together in a great body, either upon a civil or religious account." It is an assembly that gathered for worship, war, weddings, and witness of the law.
- *Ekklesia* is a combination of two Greek words, which mean "to call out". This word appears about 80 times in the singular and 35 times in the plural throughout scripture.

Thomas Oden, in his 1998 academic <u>Systematic Theology 3: Life In The Spirit</u>, posits that the apostles used the word *ekklesia* to refer to the act of gathering or assemblage of persons brought together by the Lord's own calling for the purpose of hearing the gospel and sitting at the table with the Living God. Thus, when we specifically examine these words, we can understand how they provide more accuracy in defining the concept of church. *Ekklesia* was also used in a political context to describe a special cabinet of delegates chosen by the chief governor, empowered for service. This means that those who are a part of the *ekklesia* have been granted the power of attorney to act on behalf of their King and Kingdom. Consequently, the church is the official representative of the Kingdom of God upon the earth.

How important is the church? Well, the church is the most important organism upon the earth. While Christ, Himself, only refers to it twice, He lays claim as its owner. The New Testament writers, however, make mention of the church about nearly 100 times. Paul frames the church in the book of Ephesians as the body and bride of Christ. Christ is the head, which means He thinks for the body — He is the brain (Ephesians 1:22-23). The church, therefore, is to have the same mentality that He has (Philippians 2:5). The church cannot make decisions independent of His established doctrinal thought; it exists to reflect His wishes, His will, and His ways. Without His mind, it dies or ceases being relevant.

Paul used the scenario in the Garden of Eden to allegorize the church (Ephesians 5:22-32). He describes Adam as a type of Christ and his sleep as a type of crucifixion. He sees Eve as a type of church, and He sees Adam's side as the birth place of the church and the mandate to be fruitful and multiply as the call of the church to evangelism and discipleship. The sole purpose of the church is to represent the Kingdom of God and make disciples that in turn will serve in the church that is simply a reflection of Christ's Kingdom.

The same allegory is also in Saint Augustine's classic 5th century treatise, <u>City of God</u>. He describes the garden as the church itself, the four rivers in the garden as the four gospels and fruit bearing trees as the saints themselves. Fruits are their works, the tree of life is Christ, the tree of the knowledge of good and evil represents our free will choices. When we examine the garden scenario and research historical biblical literature, it is clear that the early church fathers (Patristics), theologians and scholars have always recognized the purpose of the church. *The church is important.* The church is promised in Matthew 16, where Christ says that upon this rock I will build My church. It was planted in Acts, when the Lord added to the church daily (Acts 2:47), and its destiny was prophesied in Ephesians 5:27, where it states that Christ will present to Himself a glorious church without defect.

At its inception, the Church in the New Testament was not a social institution. It was an organism that saw itself on a spiritual mission. When we examine the apostolic church or early church, as it was birthed in the 1st century church, you see a church that was consumed with the Great Commission in Jerusalem, Judea, Samaria, and the outer most parts of the world. In Acts 28:3-28, the last verses in the book of Acts focus on Paul residing in a rented house teaching the things concerning Christ and the Kingdom of God. Without question, the church Jesus Christ created was intended to reflect the Kingdom of God and be a transforming agency upon the earth. But the church was not to be synonymous with contemporary culture. Great men have attempted to address this issue of Christ and culture throughout the ages. The question of the church's role and purpose has always been a long-standing question in Christendom.

Fuellenbach suggests that the church serves the Kingdom by spreading the Gospel's values throughout the world in an expression of the Kingdom and that it assists people in accepting God's plan.[6] Early church father Cyprian states that there is no salvation outside the church.[7] Why? Because the church is the designated vehicle God uses to usher people into the Kingdom —God's covenant representative upon the earth during the Church Age. The church, according to Romans 11:11-36, has become the spiritual Israel. The church has assumed the role that Israel had in the Old Testament. It now represents God upon the earth. The church consists, not of a race belonging to Abraham, but an elected race whose progenitor is Christ, the father of the Christian faith.

When an apostle established a local church, it served as a pillar of truth in that area. The apostle wrote letters to the local churches to guide and direct their actions and problems. These letters were not written and sent to only one specific church, but to every body of believers in a particular place. It didn't go to the "1st Corinthian church of the newborn sanctified holiness movement" only, but it was circulated to all the churches in Corinth. There was one message to every church because every church was expected to be an outpost of the Kingdom of God, responsible for creating fully functioning disciples of Christ in its locality and supporting the apostolic vision of reaching Jerusalem, Judea, Samaria, and the uttermost parts of the world with the Kingdom gospel. They were organized from house to house according to Acts 15:4, Acts 15: 22, and Acts 18:22 and reflected the wishes of the Jerusalem church. [See also Acts 11:22; Acts 15:6-29.] The early church was absolutely consumed with discipling the world! That is why we see Paul soliciting financial support so that he can launch out in his missionary journeys.

A real life example of the relationship between the church and the Kingdom is found in our governmental relationships with foreign countries. In the countries where the United States has a national interest, our nation requests and maintains an outpost called an embassy. The embassy acts as the official representative of the United States of America in that foreign country. If an American traveling abroad is on the soil or in the territory of the embassy, he can enjoy the same laws, privileges, and treatment that he would enjoy in America proper. The embassy's responsibilities are to issue legal entry into America, to educate the foreign country on the culture of America, to educate visiting Americans on the culture of the people native to that country, and to protect any Americans living in the foreign country.

The church should function as an embassy of the Kingdom of God. With the authority of the Kingdom, the church is the vehicle by which the world hears and receives the Gospel of Jesus Christ. In essence, the business of the church is expansion of the Kingdom of God in a foreign land. A person must be born again in order to enter the Kingdom, but once they are born into the Kingdom, the embassy or the church is where all Kingdom citizens meet, worship, learn about God, become equipped for ministry, and empowered to be a witness for Christ. The ministry of the embassy is reconciliation. People are given life in the Kingdom and equipped for ministry in the church!

Just like our modern-day governmental models, each embassy has an ambassador, the pastor (Ephesians 6:20, 2 Corinthians 5:20) and we are 'ministers' of reconciliation (2 Corinthians 5:18). Paul refers to himself as an ambassador and those who serve in the embassy as ministers of foreign affairs. The role of the ambassador is to equip the saints for the work of ministry, according to Ephesians 4:12. Therefore, when we look at the Kingdom of God as our homeland and the church as the embassy, the embassy's role is to reconnect a fallen humanity to the King. But somehow the embassy began to reflect the country in which it was established, and the "church doors" became an entry way to a place that has nothing to do with the Kingdom of God.

The early church was under constant persecution because of the aggressive fulfillment of its purpose as Christ's embassy, constantly speaking out on and promoting the cause and the authority of Christ and His Kingdom. They did this in the face of a dominant, allegiance-demanding Roman Empire, as well as a jealous, derisive Jewish religion and culture. The church was continually under severe, condoned persecution for representing Christ as the King, which was an offense to both the Jews and the Romans. (Acts 8:1, Acts 8:3, and Acts 12:1)

In addition to reconciliation, the embassy was responsible for leadership development, intercession, and instruction. (Acts 11:26, Acts 12:5, Acts 13:1, Acts 14:23, and Acts 20:28) The New Testament church *taught* the Kingdom of God. Therefore, the role of the church according to the book of Acts, which records the actions of the apostles, was to represent Christ to the nations from Jerusalem to the uttermost parts of the world. The church was not designed to reflect the culture in which it existed. It reflected a unique but unpopular departure from civilized society: the culture of the Kingdom of God. Thus, the church was not inviting people into the church; it were inviting people into the Kingdom.

What was the original physical structure of the embassy in the 1st century? It was what we'd call a house church; and the house was literally an embassy, a refuge where the Kingdom culture could be openly and freely expressed, encouraged, and edified. And each man's house represented the domain or the territory of God. That's the reason Christian homes were administrated according to apostolic order, because the house was all they had. People didn't espouse one thing in public worship and enact another at home. Worship and home were identical.

In Christianity, the embassy started in a house and after establishing apostolic order or official offices of the church: Apostles, Prophets, Evangelists, Pastors, and Teachers, who were also elders of the church, the Lord added to the embassy daily. It is imperative for us to understand that when we receive Christ as our Lord and Savior, He then hands us over to the church and includes us in the society called the Body of Christ. In Christ's 'society', He is the head of His Body, or His Church.

The Scripture also states, "And believers were increasingly added to the *Lord*, multitudes of both men and women," (Acts 5:14). In Acts 2:47, they were added to the church and in Acts 5:14, they were added to the Lord. Also, the Word of God spread and the number of disciples multiplied greatly. Then the churches were multiplied according to Acts 9:31:

> *"Then the churches throughout all Judea, Galilee, and Samaria had peace and were edified. And walking in the fear of the Lord and in the comfort of the Holy Spirit, they were multiplied."*

The book of Acts outlines a logical progression of tasks within each embassy that expands the embassy network. Acts 2:41 states that 3,000 were *added* in one day, and in verse 47 more were being added daily. Then in Acts 5:14, the embassy recruits for the Lord because it states that they added to the Lord. God gives a foundation for the embassy and then the embassy starts adding to the Lord. Then the progression moves to Acts 6 and 7 where now those that were added to the Lord are being *discipled*. The progression then moves to Acts 9:31 where the disciples multiplied embassies, which means now they began to *multiply churches*. These verses describe how the Body of Christ reached Jerusalem, Judea, Samaria, and the uttermost parts of the world. We have to proclaim the Kingdom, receive the Lord's additions to the embassy, make them disciples, and then multiply embassies. It is up to you to spread the gospel of the Kingdom.

The Emergence of Church Doors

The primary purpose of the church is reconciliation and disciple-making. Everyone that is a part of the Body of Christ is expected to live as Kingdom citizens and work in the church, so we all appear to live in the Kingdom and work in the church! But with the rise of the mega-church, it may look as if that's what good Christians are doing—but looks are deceiving. Also, the explosive growth of the international multi-media means that spreading the gospel of Jesus Christ worldwide can lend itself to that impression. Unfortunately, national statistics bear out the truth: we are being totally ineffective as witnesses for the Kingdom of God and we are not bringing people to Christ and into the church in America. We're lagging behind churches and sects all over the world. As a matter of fact, statistics show that in the course of a year it takes 85 Christians to bring one convert to Christ in the American Christian Church.[8]

Current statistics show that increasing numbers of Americans, almost one-fifth of our entire population, say they are unaffiliated with any religious group or tradition.[9] The church has lost its appeal, its fire, its passion – and growing numbers of our population do not want to come. Now can you understand why the church is losing three to four thousand churches a year in America? The church no longer reflects God's wishes, God's will, and God's ways. It is no longer governed by the mind of Christ. This is not the church that Jesus built – there is a counterfeit on the earth. And this counterfeit has put doors on the church.

There is nothing inherently wrong with an inanimate object called a door; but architecturally, doors perform a function. A door provides access or participation, and it acts as a barrier to entry. My question is this: where did this *door* come from? Who was the architect and who was the locksmith?

The Bible never teaches that Christ's church had a door – the Lord added to the church those that were being saved. Period. And the Bible does not teach that believers have keys to the church. The Bible teaches that we have been given the keys to the Kingdom of heaven. So I want to know, where the reality of this door has come from. And who distributed the keys to *it*? Who opened *that* door? Furthermore, on whose authority were the "doors of the church" opened? At what point did the keys to the Kingdom of heaven become the keys to the doors of the church? Most significantly, who said that we were to usher people into the church? Somewhere throughout the course of history, a human being either innocently bastardized or egotistically commandeered God's invitation to the unbeliever. The implied ownership of the church, which has obviously taken place based on the social hi-jacking of God's domain that we see in all quarters of Christendom, is emblazoned in the declaration that the "doors of the church" were open. But is anyone able to open the doors of the church when Jesus said He is the way the truth and the life no man come to the Father but by Him? How can the church doors be opened when Jesus is the door?! Someone decided to take the Lord's church and give it a new vision and mission!

This means that there is a counterfeit, secularized, humanistic new church that has created doors to Jesus' assembly and opened them for *member*ship. A review of Christian church history indicates that the doors of the church were actually opened in 313 A.D. with the signing of the Edict of Milan.[10] According to the online New Catholic Dictionary, the Edict was granted by the Emperors Constantine the Great in the West and Licinius in the East; it bestowed religious freedom throughout the Roman Empire and the proclamation permanently established religious toleration of Christianity. After more than two centuries of intense, intermittent persecution of Christians, many of whom were marked with particular cruelty and murdered for sport, the edict meant much more than toleration. There was also increased political pressure to recognize the growing ranks of converts due to the threat Christianity posed to the state government.

The Edict of Milan, marking the authoritative recognition of Christianity as an authentic religion, was a political agreement specifying the following by the Emperors: an end to Christian persecution and restoration of their churches, cemeteries, and other property that the state had confiscated. Though the toleration was agreed upon jointly with Licinius, Constantine led the movement to bestow full freedom upon the church and to make Christianity the official religion of the Roman Empire. The Edict of Milan was signed because Constantine said that he had a vision that Christianity could give him victory on the battlefield. He put the Greek letters representing the first two letters for Christ, or Christos, on all of his soldiers' shields and they triumphed in battle. Constantine then gave the Christian God the credit for the victory, declared Rome a Christian empire and became the official emperor of all of Rome.

The apostolic church of the first century was consumed with the message of the Kingdom, the Patristic Fathers would all be turning over in their graves if they saw how the doors of the church were "opened." Prior to the Edict, the church was not publicly recognized as a viable institution upon the earth because its very presence threatened the authority of the king of this world. Christians could be put to death for calling Jesus Christ Lord. So every emperor, every king, and every governmental official felt intimidated by the Christian presence because they understood that the church was trying to recruit people to a Kingdom that was not theirs. So, when the early church worshipped, they had to gather in catacombs, a system of caves, and other hidden places. Initially, they could not exist on the same turf with the Roman governmental authorities, while having separate, public agendas, which were mutually exclusive.

Constantine the Great opened the doors of the Imperial Church in 323 AD and began the period that I refer to as "the doors of the church are open." Many people consider this period of time the death of Christianity and the rise of the Christian religion because many, if not most, were "converted" by way of the sword. Sunday was declared a day of observance for worship, due in part to the beginnings of secular blending into the doctrine of Christianity. Prior to this time, Constantine was a solar henotheist, believing in one God, while not denying the existence of others. All work ceased on Sundays in the Roman Empire. Why? Because the doors of the church were now open. Roman citizens were fined and tortured for not "going to church" on Sunday. Philip Yancey has well said that "coziness between church and state is good for the state and bad for the church."[11]

The New Testament gathering of believers that had been meeting *"every day in the temple and at home"* (Acts 5:42) deteriorated to a Sunday-only, cathedral environment where church life became institutionalized and formal. Everybody who was anybody sought membership in the church again, primarily for sociological reasons. Those sincerely seeking the heart of God, along with social climbers seeking financial gain and status, desired membership in the Church and were admitted on equal footing. Ambitious, worldly, and unscrupulous men sought office in the church to gain social and political influence.

In the aftermath of the Edict of Milan, worldliness overtook spirituality in the church. Having a state church meant that the state controlled the church; spirituality did not influence the state. The doors of the church were mounted and swung wide open and all were allowed entry, particularly if there were financial and political gains at stake, because the Emperor governed the church. *God was no longer in charge of the church.* God never opened those doors; Constantine opened them and Constantine governed them. This era initiated the paradigm of the church as a sociological phenomenon, which was something God never intended it to be. It was also the beginning of the church's slide down the slippery slope of man-made religion; an institution with clear socialization goals mutated into an organism in which Christ's original message of the Kingdom of God became subservient to the will of the State.

After the creation of the Imperial Church, the church was constantly in the throes of reform. The Protestant Reformation, begun in 1517 when Martin Luther posted his 95 Theses, openly criticized the Pope and the Roman Catholic Church. This is the church that evolved from Emperor Constantine's state church twelve centuries earlier. This movement was an attempt to modify or reform the church and rectify the travesty of the church's departure from its roots and its purpose. However, the Roman Catholic Church rejected reformation, and the state church's refusal to change gave way to the Protestant movement in Europe, which later inspired the Great Awakenings in the United States, beginning in the early 18th century. Reformation was, and always will be, necessary in order to maintain the spiritual integrity of the church. Why? Because over time, men tend to allow their traditions to nullify the Word of God (Matthew 15:8).

Traditionalism is what caused Israel to stray from God; it so clouded their vision that they could not recognize the long awaited Messiah. When Christ came, the Law of Moses had become diluted by the traditions of Israel. The law was supposed to atone for the sins of Israel but the leaders created additional books to govern the tribes. Over time, Israel was governed primarily by the Mishnah, which is the oral traditions of the rabbis that was expounded on by its highly detailed commentary, the Talmud.

John the Baptizing One came announcing the coming reformation that would result from the ministry of Jesus Christ. His message was "Repent, for the Kingdom of heaven is at hand!" Christ intended, much like Martin Luther and the other reformers, to reform Judaism and move them back toward God, but He was rejected. This rejection brought about the ultimate plan of God to include the Gentile world, thus representing another divine dispensation.

As Europeans came to America, the doors of the church were also opened here. The Church of England established its missionary arm, The Society for the Propagation of the Gospel in Foreign Parts, which granted permission for the official beginning or the foundation of the church in America in 1701. [Rabiteau, Slave Religion: The Invisible Institution in the Antebellum South: Oxford Univ. Press 1978] The Society's intent was to travel to the colonies and evangelize whites, Indians, and Africans. They wanted to expand the Kingdom to all men. However, the plantation slave owners had a problem with Christianity spreading into their new territory because of its views concerning brotherhood. Christianity promoted an equalitarian system that prohibited one Christian from enslaving another Christian. Christians taught that you could not enslave a baptized brother. The only way for the Society to get Christianity ordained as a religion in America was to accommodate the racist sentiments of the existing power structure and status quo that excluded blacks. All of these doctrinal concessions were predicated upon slavery laws. In order to appease the troubled minds of American Christians surrounding slavery, the United States government redefined an African as three-fifths of a man – less than human, thereby unqualified for the application of certain Christian values. Scholars, at the beginning of the 20th century, wrote books to validate this principle, e.g., C. Carol's book, <u>The Negro: A Beast or in the Image of God?</u>" His 'scholarly' premise – the Negro was a pre-Adamite animal, a beast created on the 6th day with the animals.[12]

In sum, the foundation of a thing determines its outcome. The Christian religion that was instituted during Constantinianism created and opened the doors of the church and those doors remained open throughout the Imperial Church, the Medieval Church, the Church of the Reformation, the Church of England, and the spread of the church to the United States. The secular compromise came around full circle: in order for the American colonies to receive the Christian church on American soil, the Great Commission was compromised for wealth and power again, 14 centuries later, in order to assuage three issues of the plantation owners:

1. Hearing the gospel required time and slaves who were spending time in worship could not be economically productive.
2. Slaves who gathered in religious assemblies might begin to recognize their own strength and plot insurrections under the guise of religious instruction, leaving the slave owner personally and economically in danger.
3. If baptized, the slave would become "Christian brother" and owners would have to take them out

of slavery.[C. Eric Lincoln cite, *The Development of Black Religion*]

America chose economics over evangelism. The Society of the Propagation of the Gospel in Foreign Parts created the Doctrine of Accommodation. It was an attractive theology for American slave control that offered incentives to plantation owners who made slave children available for Christian education. The slave owners would receive tax breaks as an incentive for allowing Sunday school attendance. These are events that have been researched and historically documented.

The church in America was born out of economic gain, cultural assassination, and forfeiture of the will of Christ the King. The doors opened and reluctantly allowed people of color in. Churches became communities built upon the demands and issues that each culture faced in deciding whether to embrace the agenda of God or embrace the agenda of a particular culture. For example, the antebellum American church, for its own purpose, embraced and promoted the superiority of the white race and culture. Traditions of the state church (Roman Catholic Church) had already infused its European culture into the images and practices of Christianity.

For example, despite the fact that the Bible prohibits images, all the people in the Bible were, and continue to be, portrayed as European. Now, we know that Egypt is a part of Africa, which means that Moses grew up in Africa. There is no way that you can take the Moses, portrayed by Charlton Heston, on television and masquerade him as the Pharaoh's daughter's son. How are you going to hide a European in Africa? The only way Moses could hide in the Pharaoh's home was if he did not stand out and had a skin complexion similar to the Egyptians.

While the white church opened the doors to superiority of race and culture, the black church opened its doors to a social and civil welfare agenda as it endeavored to escape the pains of racism and advance the welfare and equality of its people. So in essence, the black church became the civil rights movement, a cultural advancement institution, not a Kingdom movement. Many Black churches today are not concerned about the Kingdom of God. Many churches of Afro-centric affiliation are simply reflecting the historical stages of development of the black church. First, there was the church on the plantation that was governed by the master and assumed European practices and customs. Next, there was what was referred to as "the bush church": meetings were in private, a part of the invisible church. Then the black church evolved into what was called "the Negro church", then it evolved into what is called the Black church. Just as with the invisible church in the bush, some African American parishioners use the church as a place to release their emotions because of the hardships and the oppressions of life. There is not a focus on integrity, or holiness, or on distinctiveness in gender. The members in many of these churches simply desire to jump and shout and if a compromised musician can play the organ to help me shout, so be it.[13]

All other cultures and their churches simply fell in line with these mutations and perversions of the Kingdom of God message. The church as a whole became reflective of the overall American culture and the race of those who attended its services. The doors of the church that were initially opened in 313 A.D. due to socio-economic reasons continued to be opened in the caste system of England and in the slavery system of America. The opening of the church doors was and is rooted in **power, money,** and **politics**. This unholy trinity has always fueled the existence of the open-door church and has caused it to develop into an institution that is no longer concerned with the Kingdom of God.

It is a shame.

It is a disgrace before God.

Think about it, beloved. So many people come into houses of God all over this country with an attitude, with arrogance and pride; they talk about their power, position, and tenure in the church as a badge of honor. They know all of the church laws and rules but don't know any scriptures. And what is most embarrassing is that they have never led anybody to the Lord. They are embarrassed to lift up their hands and shout, "Thank you Jesus! You've been good." They can't even humble themselves and get on their knees because they worry about who's looking at them. Where is salvation by grace and freedom in Jesus? The church in America—like the church in Constantine's day—has simply become a reflection of the society in which it exists.

In America, while there was certainly intended to be a separation of church and state, initially, the founding fathers were not trying to protect the state from the church, they were trying to protect the church from the state. After all, the church had been good to America, as it helped to frame and codify laws and principles of subjugation. There are benefits to being a church and a Christian in America, much like in the Constantinian era. They, too, had non-profit tax exemptions given, and clergy received tax breaks. Clergy receive these tax breaks today, but these benefits will soon be no more. Prophetically, I can see that these kinds of tax advantages will be done away with under the requirement that churches comply with what the government determines to be a 'legal non-profit'. But the stipulation will be that this government-acknowledged entity must respect the American culture and refrain from preaching against things that are legal in America — like homosexuality — in order to maintain its tax exempt status. So, if the only reason you give to your church is because of deductions, then you'd better get your heart prepared because the King wants His taxes, even if the government will not give you a penny back.

There have been crossroads in the American Christian church and at every crossroad is an ideological challenge. We have gone through the slave church of the 1600s, which was a totally controlled church. We went through Reconstruction after the Civil War, which was a very hostile period because of Jim Crow laws. We went through the Pentecostal movement, which was designed to unite the races but once again further divided the races. We went through the post-World War II church and began a quest for the secular. One of the reasons that certain denominations and certain institutions of higher learning were built was to stay competitive in the secular markets for leadership. During this time, doctoral degrees and graduate degrees were required in secular fields, and the church wanted to compete with secular fields so they began to require that the clergy have Master of Divinity degrees and this promoted the rise of the professional clergy class. Unfortunately, what was taught in the seminaries was not how to reflect the Kingdom of God, but how to reflect the state in which you serve.

America has gone through the segregated church and the classist church and now we're dealing with the motivational church, the so-called integrated church with motivational speakers. Michael Emerson of Rice University is one of the main researchers on multi-culturalism in America and in the church.[14] His research has found that eight percent of all churches and two to three percent of mainline churches in America are considered integrated. The integrated church is a myth – there is no integration. What Dr. Martin Luther King said in the 1960s still holds true today: the 11:00 o'clock worship hour is the most segregated hour in America. The only reason we work together is because the state says we have to. The only reason we eat together is because the state says we have to, but when people are left to their own choices for worship, they don't want to be around Kingdom people — they want to be around *their* kind of people. Why? Because we rally around sociological issues — carnal issues, not spiritual issues. When you are spiritual you're supposed to be closer to me, as a Christian, than to natural brothers and sisters. You see, the bond of the spirit is supposed to be closer than the bond of the flesh, but people feel safer in their cultural environments. The creation of doors to the church has effectively shut out the will and power of the Kingdom of God, as well as the mind of Christ our King.

What Has Come In and Out of the Church

What has the church historically taught through its opened doors at the expense of neglecting the Kingdom? When Constantine opened the doors of the church by making it the official religion of the Roman Empire, all kinds of doctrine, practices, festivals and structures came in the church. Unfortunately, they have been in the church for so long, people would rather abandon the truth of the gospel than their lifelong traditions. Christ spoke about the power of tradition and He declared that traditions could nullify the Word of God (Matthew 15:8). But if the Roman Empire opened the doors, then the American Church put a door stopper in it to ensure that it would never close. When we look at the practices and philosophies that have been allowed in the church versus what the Bible teaches, it is simply mind-blowing. I would like to take a little time to look at some of the things that entered the church while the doors were opened by the Roman Empire, the Church of England, and the American Colonists. The things that were allowed to enter the church were the things that forced Christ out of the church. There was a hostile take over that will leave thousands facing a Great Disappointment.

It may appear that I am being very hard, and even unfair, to the church, but the church has been under observation by men of God throughout church history. St. Augustine, Luther, Calvin, Wesley, Niebuhr and others have analyzed the church and found it lacking and attempted to reform it. Augustine, in his work entitled The City of God, divides the church into two categories — the visible and invisible. The church has been a turbulent institution since it was under the influence of the Roman Empire. Prior to its marriage to Rome, the church was an institution that focused upon spreading the message of Christ and the Kingdom of God. Has there been any good that has come out of the church since the Roman wedding? Of course! The church has and is still producing people that love God, but the majority of the churches, especially in America, are not producing disciples for Christ; they are creating financial support for debt servicing and lavish living. Don't misunderstand me — there are people getting saved in the church and undergoing personal transformation, even the Roman Catholic Church. However, it is due to neither the vision nor the context of the church; it is due to the level of aggression of the individual.

Still, the church has provided many of us a platform for salvation and service, many of us would not have a relationship with Christ today had it not been for our exposure to and experience with the church. The problem is that the church that led us to Christ has lost its focus and appeal, and the spirit of the age has taken hold of it and has led it into captivity. The church, as I see it, has been exiled into Roman captivity. Martin Luther, during his reformation, saw the church being exiled into what he called, Babylonian captivity, which was where Israel was robbed of its culture, worship, language, and focus. In the same fashion, Roman captivity produced an environment for Christians to practice their religion as vassals of the Roman Empire. Roman dominion created a classist level of clergy that learned to partner with the government in order to earn favors; this group was similar to the Sanhedrin in Jewish society (Pharisees and Sadducees). Today, the Christian church is endeavoring to be politically correct in a corrupt society and trying not to disrupt the governmental favors of tax benefits and faith-based initiatives. The church has become something it was not designed to be through dispensational development or evolutionary changes in culture and society. The Christian Church has become dislocated and disconnected from its foundation.

The doors of the church were opened, or allowed to extend membership, without persecution, pressure, or conversion. Entrance into the church was a matter of civil rights and governmental support and did not require an experience with Christ. The doors of the church have extended membership from 313AD until now, which was never in the will of God. We have opened the doors of the church and created self-proclaimed Christians, who are now simply waiting for their heavenly rewards. All kinds of elements have come through the doors of the church. For example, during this period, Constantine began building new church facilities referred to as basilicas. He consecrated pagan temples and made them churches even though they would still, from time to time, offer pagan sacrifices. He also began to give endowments to churches, money granted by the state to build. He granted privileges to clergy by exempting them from taxes and considering them as a privileged class. Clergy soon were above the law and whenever there was a dispute or legal issue that involved them, it didn't go to regular court but to a special court called an "ecclesiastical court." Does any of this sound familiar?

Pagan feasts were incorporated into liturgies and celebrated in the church with the names of the deities changed to give them more Christian significance. The negative connotation associated with the concept of the crucifixion was abolished and the cross was made a positive symbol. Images of the saints appeared in the church and were adored and worshipped. Adoration of the Virgin Mary was substituted for the worship of Venus and Diana. The Lord's Supper, which was to be done in remembrance of Christ, evolved from a memorial to a sacrifice. Thus, when the Lord's Supper is taken in the Roman Catholic Church, the wine and wafer become the literal body and blood of Jesus because of the intentional association with sacrifices made to pagan gods by the priests. And the office of an elder or the five fold ministry gifts of Ephesians 4 morphed into the role of a priest. Clearly, *the doors of the church were opened!*

All of these extra traditions are the result of the doors of the church being opened. The historical practices that were integrated set the stage for untransformed mindsets and traditions to come in with them. Below, I attempt to list some of the major elements that came through the doors of the church, but the list is not exhaustive. Suffice it to say that most of the traditions we cherish, in whatever church you belong, are *not* rooted in the Bible. That should alarm you. John, the beloved disciple, gives us a history of the church era or dispensation in Revelation 2-3.

Hold onto your seat! I am about to teach from the dreaded and avoided book of Revelation. The sociological church rarely teaches from the book of Revelation; in fact, as a fresh, new pastor I was counseled to do two things: preach happy, encouraging messages and never use the book of Revelation. However, by taking a panoramic view of the seven churches described in Revelation, we get a bird's eye view of what has led to the doors of the church opening and what came in and out of its doors. The seven churches of Asia Minor give us some clues of the dispensations and transitions of the church age. Each of the seven churches described in Revelation has significance that is both existential and eschatological (pertaining to the end times prophecies). This dual signifi- cance suggests that the church was literally going through what the text indicates at that time, as well as what the church would experience in the future — its prophetic significance. An examination of the seven churches gives us both historic and prophetic insight into the church age. The age that is to come is referred to as Daniel's 70th week or the Tribulation period.

What has come in and out of the doors of the church? We can examine the historical significance of the church by closely looking at the seven churches. Tim La Haye, in his book, Revelation, gives list of particulars that I will reference as we consider what has come in and out of the doors of the church and its impact. John, the author of the book of Revelation, lists both the positives and the negatives of every church age, which serve as a biblical basis to examine what has come in and out of the doors of the church historically and prophetically.

The church of Ephesus: The Apostolic church, 30-100 AD. This is the church that we see in the book of Acts worshipping both in the house and the temple; it is the Kingdom-driven church, the church of revelation.

- Commendation: I know your works, your labor, your patience, and that you cannot bear those who are evil. And you have tested those who say they are apostles and are not, and have found them liars; and you have persevered and have patience, and have labored for My name's sake and have not become weary. (Revelation 2:2,3)
- Condemnation: Remember therefore from where you have fallen; repent and do the first works (Revelation 2:5)

The church at Smyrna: The Persecuted church, 100-312AD. This church experienced the greatest time of persecution in its history.

- Commendation: I know your works, tribulation, and poverty (but you are rich) (Revelation 2:9)
- Condemnation: Not a word!

Satan tried to exterminate the church due to the apostolic church's effectiveness at preaching the Kingdom. One church historian estimates that during this period five million Christians were martyred for the testimony of Christ. The church of Smyrna is the church that was persecuted for its faithfulness to the mission of spreading the message of God's Kingdom. It was prophesied that they would have persecution for 10 days, but if they would be faithful unto death, they would be given a crown. Ten, in biblical numerology, is the number of redemption; after ten periods of persecution, God promised a time of redemption or peace. This is the final period before the doors of the church would be opened and the ability to practice one's faith free from persecution was available. Church history gives us exactly 10 periods where 10 evil emperors led persecutions against Christians before the transition.

Table 1.1

Nero	AD 54 - 68	Paul beheaded and Peter crucified
Domitian	AD 81 - 96	John exiled
Trajan	AD 98 - 117	Ignatius burned at the stake

Marcus Aurelius	AD 161 - 180	Justin the martyr killed
Severus	AD 193 - 211	
Maximinius	AD 235 - 238	
Decius	AD 249 - 251	
Valerian	AD 253 - 260	
Aurelian	AD 270 - 275	
Diocletian	AD 284 - 305	

The church of Pergamos: The Indulged church, 312-606 AD. Pergamos was a city given to the worship of many Greek idols.

- Commendation: And you hold fast to My name, and did not deny My faith, even amidst persecution. (Revelation 2:13)
- Condemnation: You have there those who hold the doctrine of Balaam, who taught Balak to put a stumbling block before the children of Israel, to eat things sacrificed to idols, and to commit sexual immorality. Thus you also have those who hold the doctrine of the Nicolaitans, which thing I hate. (Revelation 2:14,15)

It is said that Pergamos was the city of Satan's throne. Satan has a kingdom and Babylon had, from earlier times, been considered the capital of this kingdom. Idolatry, under the inspiration of Satan, began during the reign of King Nimrod and his mother. After the decline of Babylon, it is believed that Satan established his headquarters in Pergamos because of its strong idolatrous religions. This is the church age where Satan attains his strongest position in the church (Revelation 2:13).

This era also includes the period of time that the doors of the church were first opened; now we can take a historical perspective at what came into the church under the Roman Empire. Pagan practices entered into the church as a return of favor to the emperor for the Edict of toleration, or Milan. The following were introduced to the church during this period:

1. prayers for the dead (300 AD)
2. making a sign of the cross (300 AD)
3. worship of saints and angels (375 AD)
4. mass first instituted (394 AD)
5. worship of Mary begun (431 AD)
6. priest began dressing differently then laymen (500 AD)
7. extreme unction, anointing the sick, last rites - for preparation of death (526 AD)
8. doctrine of purgatory (593 AD)
9. worship service introduced in Latin (600 AD)
10. prayers directed to Mary (600 AD)

From 312 AD on, the church became more Roman and less Christian in its practices. The Roman Catholic Church is hard pressed to trace its roots back further than Constantine, however, beyond that, the church was a collection of independent gatherings with no central authority. The name Pergamos means, "marriage" or "elevation". The church became married to governmental authority and elevated to a place of acceptance. This church era was the beginning of the end of the power and spirituality of the church and rather than being an institution that represented God, it began to represent the Roman Empire as a state religion.

The church of Thyatira: The Pagan church, 606 AD to the tribulation.

- Commendation: I know your works, love, service, faith, and your patience; and as for your works, the last are more than the first. (Revelation 2:19)
- Condemnation: You allow that woman Jezebel, who calls herself a prophetess, to teach and seduce My servants to commit sexual immorality and eat things sacrificed to idols. (Revelation 2:20)

This era introduced many of the mystical practices of the East into the church such as:

1. Boniface made the first Pope (607 AD)
2. kissing the Pope's foot (709 AD)
3. worshipping images and relics (786 AD)
4. use of "holy water" (850 AD)
5. canonization of the dead saints (995 AD)
6. celibacy of the priesthood (1079 AD)
7. prayer beads (1090 AD)
8. sale of indulgences (1190 AD)
9. transubstantiation (1215 AD)
10. adoration of the wafer (1220 AD)
11. Bible forbidden to laymen (1229 AD)
12. cup forbidden to people at communion (1414 AD)
13. tradition granted equal authority with Bible (1545 AD)
14. apocrypha put in Bible (1546 AD)
15. infallibility of the Pope (1870 AD)
16. public schools condemned (1930 AD)

These are just a few things that came through the door during this period! Works righteousness is the over-arching characteristic of this church that extends even into the contemporary church. The Roman Catholic Church opened the door to a new Judeo-Christian Judaism – traditions designed to prove a believer's worthiness to themselves and others.

The church of Sardis: The Dead church, 1520 – tribulation.

- Commendation: I know your works, that you have a name that you are alive, (Revelation 3:1)
- Condemnation: But you are dead. (Revelation 3:1)

The name Sardis means 'escaping ones' or 'those who come out.' This is the church of the Reformation, to whom God said that while its efforts were admirable, it was still considered a dead church. The Reformation movement did not guide the church to radical change; it simply shook some things up. The Lutheran Church eventually became the state church of Germany due to the political compromise of Martin Luther. The fact that the Lutheran church became a state church meant there was no need for conversion to be a part of the church, thus it was dead. Political favors came through the doors of the church. Many politicians greased the hands of the leadership of a church and caused the church to be ineffective in its spiritual agenda. Church and politics simply don't mix. Now don't get me wrong, every member of the church should vote and be active part of the democratic process of selecting governmental leaders. But when politics enters into the church, the church may become publicly successful but spiritually irrelevant. The church of the Reformation continued many of the practices of the Roman Catholic Church that were not rooted in scripture but embedded in the culture of the people. Opening the doors of the church vs. opening the gates to the Kingdom moved people to influence God's house but ignore God's reign.

The church of Philadelphia: the church that Christ loved, 1750 to the Rapture (the great snatching away described in 1 Thessalonians 4:17).

- Commendation: I know your works. See, I have set before you an open door, and no one can shut it; for you have a little strength, have kept My word, and have not denied My name. (Revelation 3:8)
- Condemnation: Not a word!

This is the church of the Great Awakening. This church ensured that people had a personal experience with God. The Great Awakening era involved the likes of George Whitefield, Jonathan Edwards, John Wesley and others. This movement was responsible for great revivals in Europe, from the British Isles to America. This church was granted an open door to lead missionary movements that touched the world with the gospel. This movement spread through men such as William Carey to India, Africa, China, Japan, Korea, South America, and the Islands of the sea.

The Bible states that this church will make known those who say they are from the house of Israel but are not and are from the synagogue of Satan. Since the church of Philadelphia still exists today, this church makes clear the waywardness of the church that calls herself the church but has become the synagogue of Satan. Because of the perseverance of this church, they will be kept from the hour of trial. This hour of trial refers to the Tribulation period John wrote about in the book of Revelation, often referred to as Daniel's 70th week. They are promised to be removed quickly before the world suffers. But until that time comes, this church is doing everything within its power to usher people into the Kingdom. This church is constantly trying to spread the gospel, and even though great challenges threaten its efforts, this church endeavors to walk through the open door. (Revelation 3:10) She will be a part of the New Jerusalem!

This church has some important characteristics:

1. Christ is seen as the one who holds a key and who opens and shuts doors that no one can open or shut. Thus, it gives us the indication that this era is about opening and closing doors.
2. This is the remnant church that exists along side the dominant church but has experienced Christ the King as holy, true, and authoritative.
3. He that has complete access to God. (Key of David)

The Church of Laodicea: The Apostate church, the people's church, 1900-tribulation.

- Commendation: Not a word!
- Condemnation: I know your works, that you are neither cold nor hot. I could wish you were cold or hot. So then, because you are lukewarm, and neither cold nor hot, I will vomit you out of My mouth. Because you say, 'I am rich, have become wealthy, and have need of nothing'—and do not know that you are wretched, miserable, poor, blind, and naked.

The seventh church leaves Christ voted out of the church and knocking on a closed door. By reviewing church history, we see a progression through the seven churches that culminates with the doors of the church being closed. The next scenario is the Rapture as pictured in Revelation, chapter 4. So please note, beloved, the Laodicean church is the last church before the Rapture and Jesus' counsel to them is to hear His voice, open the door and dine with Him!

So, what came in and out of the doors of the church before they were closed?

- Discernment: when we look at the seven churches that represent the entire church age, we see that two churches do not receive condemnations from Christ: the church of Smyrna, the Persecuted church, and the church of Philadelphia, the Missionary church. The common characteristic of both of these churches is that they are both Great Commission-oriented. They are not state churches, driven by politics and capital gain. These churches are churches of risk, their mission can and did cost them their lives. Both of these churches have little strength or lack political backing but both persevere. And both of these churches must contend with the synagogue of Satan, which is church of counterfeit Christians. These synagogues of Satan are so-called believers that claim connection to God, but blaspheme Him and do not worship (Revelation 2:9 and Revelation 3:9).
- Disciples: Study of the seven churches shows us that there are those who overcome in every dispensation.
- Doctrine: During the Roman church era, the church was allowed to stabilize her beliefs and out of the church doors came:
- Nicaea: Christology, (324-5 AD)
- Constantinople: Pneumatology, (381 AD)
- Council of Carthage: the Bible, (397 AD)
- The Patristic teachings: Athanasius, Three Capadocians, Augustine, Ambrose, Chrysostom, Jerome, etc. The Trinity (Basil of Caesarea, Gregory of Nyssa, Gregory of Nazianzus)
- Ephesus: Christology, (431 AD)
- Chalcedon: the two natures of Christ - human and divine, (451 AD)

- Despair: monasteries developed due to compromise of the church
- Disgrace: crusades for Christianity; which involved murder, rape, and all kinds of evil; sexism; witch hunts; slavery, and the exploitation of Africa in the name of God and the Pope (1441 AD).
- Disconnection from God: the priest, the language, the Bible, and communion/baptism lost all personal touch, taught people how to be Christians without intimacy and scripture
- Disillusionment: Reformist lost hope in God through the church
- Demonic activities: taught witchcraft and rebellion in the church, necromancing, fortune telling, astrology, Eastern mysticism, etc.

Doors are used for both entry and exit, opportunities and obstacles. The opening of the doors of the church during the Roman Empire created one reality for the church and the perpetuation of the doors being open in America created another reality. The church doors in America welcomed another wave of cultism and a counterfeit theology in the church. With each church era mentioned, each church became the foundation or transition into the next church age. While the transitions took place, some of the traits of the previous church age remained and fed into the next age. The church of the revivalist or the Great Awakening was a church that constantly challenged the mentality of the American church. John Wesley on multiple occasions wrote fiery letters to the American Church about slavery and how it violated the Word of God. He was a part of the church of Philadelphia (missionary church). The church of Philadelphia is a body of zealous people for God that are not a part of the mainstream mentality of the church, thus they are in a class of their own.

However, we know that the Laodicean Church is the ultimate end of the church and their attitude represents a combination of the evil foundations of the previous churches that Christ spoke negatively of. When we examine the development of the mainstream church, the fabric of its practices is based upon the compromise of Pergamos, the corruption of Thyatira, and the deadness of Sardis. And the conclusion is, "We no longer need you, Jesus; we have been around here long enough as an institution and don't need you cramping our style". So we have now what St. Augustine referred to as the visible and the invisible church. We have two strands of the people of God, thus who are listening to His voice and coming out and those who have refused to repent for so long, they can no longer recognize His voice. The Laodicean Church is responsible for ultimately locking Christ out, but allowing other things in. It is a church that suffers from several ailments:

1. moral compromise or situational ethics
2. miserable membership, tired of church politics and emotional and psychological problems
3. spiritual apathy
4. lack of spiritual vision and perception
5. uncovered by God but doesn't realize it
6. prosperity derived from the merchandising of people.

This church has allowed racism, classism, sexism, denominationalism, and idolatry through its doors. In the name of becoming a prosperous nation, it corrupted the church by using the church for financial and political gain. In the same way that the church has historically compromised doctrine for the sake of secular advancement, the church of Laodicea sold its very soul and no longer has a valid identity — it is naked! The church in America had its beginning in the 1700's during slavery's heyday. When given an opportunity to embrace the new African immigrants as brothers, the American church instead sided with government and chose economics over evangelism.

One of the most deadly elements that has come through the doors of the church has been the creation and acceptance of European images depicting Jesus and others in the Bible, effecting the murder of the Jewish culture of Christ. False images came into the church as a result of allowing the spirit of racism and cultural superiority in the foundation of the American church. And by essentially rewriting history in the minds of the people, the Europeans' economic agenda of colonization was bolstered. The spirit of European idol worship was promoted through the church, while also supporting the evil deeds of colonization in the name of God. The abuse of women came through this same door and this sexist spirit continues to devalue the role of women in the home and in the church.

Our society determines the value of people according to their class group and their ethnicity; in the same fashion, the church is divided along the lines of race and class. While most non-blacks will swear up and down that they are not racist and their best friends are black, they will not join a ministry under black leadership. Is it because black preachers are inferior? Of course not, the fabric of our nation teaches whites that blacks need to stay with blacks and whites need to stay with whites; but as the subordinate class, blacks can learn from whites, but blacks cannot teach anything to whites. These words are never articulated but something about whites being under black leadership is 'not right'. Deep in American culture, we still hold onto the vestiges of the laws that prohibited the fraternization of the races. The only time fraternization was allowed was to the benefit of whites. The spirit of racism, exacerbated by our history of slavery, has created fear in the minds of non-blacks. In the end, the spirit of racism, classism, sexism, and denominationalism have done as much harm to the Protestant church as the medieval pagan practices did to the Roman Catholic Church. Because Christianity was misrepresented, we have groups, like the nation of Islam, who have refused to embrace Christianity because they know that the sociological church has been contaminated and that within it, blacks and whites will forever be separated and never equal. Unfortunately, many of the truths about both world and Christian history have been ignored by the church while the rest of the world knows the truth.

I can hear the voices of the detractors: "We do have some integrated churches!" When I was writing my last dissertation, which focused on multiculturalism in the Christian Church, I discovered that one of the greatest statisticians and researchers on integration in the Christian Church lived right in Houston, Texas - Michael Emerson. Michael Emerson and his group found that less than three percent of all the Christian churches in America are integrated. And they define integration by having 30 percent of another group other than the majority race. When they researched the kinds of leadership that existed in so-called integrated churches, very little, if any of that leadership, included people of African-American descent. Normally, leadership was European and or some race other than African-American.

Mr. Emerson concluded that what seems like integration has been deemed unhealthy for its participants. This is because the minority individuals who become a part of the majority church have to pay a tremendous price in cultural experience because they are taught that their own relatives are not worth continuing to fellowship with. They have to pay a heck of a price. Eventually, they found that minorities in the so-called integrated churches end up leaving, but the statistics remain the same because there is such a pull for minorities to go to majority churches. These churches are changing their minority faces, the people are not staying but it looks like integration because when one person leaves, another fills his spot.

The problem is that, across the entire landscape of the church, all of the interaction is moving in one direction – minority to majority. And when everything is moving in one direction, we cannot consider that to be integration, influenced by the Spirit of God, especially when you consider the history of our nation and the church. We must stop trying to appeal to people based upon cultural affiliations and affections. God is going to deal once again with this false spirit of integration in the church, which is nothing more than a cloak for the superiority of Euro-centrism.

Assimilation is not the answer either; God is not calling for us all to be alike, but for us to respect our differences without condescension. I have seen white parents and their children ridicule the worship style of an expressive black church as though it is a sub-church culture. In reality, the worship style of Africans reflect more of the worship style in the Bible than does white worship styles because of Christianity's Afro-Asiatic and Judaic roots. (NOTE: I do acknowledge that there are denominational churches, whether black or white, that do not reflect a scripturally-based worship style. The spirit of racism has made this a cultural issue when it's really a Kingdom issue.) We have allowed elements to enter the church and prevent the unification of the races, which Pentecost (the advent of the Holy Spirit) was meant to accomplish.

You may be asking, "Is church relevant? Is it a negative thing to go to church? I thought the church was a valid organization." These are very good questions and when you consider the information that we discussed based upon dispensationalism, the Seven Dispensations of Theological Renewal and the historical dispensations of the church based upon Revelation chapters two and three, these are critical questions. As we consider the historical and prophetic messages of the seven churches of Asia Minor, they give us great insight concerning the above mentioned questions. According to John's writing there were only two churches of the seven that did not receive a word of condemnation. The two churches that only received commendation void of condemnation were the Church of Smyrna and the Church of Philadelphia. If you recall the church of Smyrna was the Persecuted church during the second and third centuries. And the church of Philadelphia was the Missionary church of the eighteenth century. This observation is extremely important to remember in order to understand the church age in which you exist and to evaluate the church you currently attend. This is not the time to be ignorant about where you are with God – we should be as wise as the children of Issachar who understood the times to know what to do (1 Chronicles 12:32).

Where are we? Let's recap the progression of thought and practice of the church age. There are five other churches that received both commendations and condemnation and these churches transform, evolve, and open the way to the next church. The early church was criticized for losing its first love. However, this church evolved into the next church age of Persecution, or Smyrna. The church of Smyrna faced intense persecution, which did not lift until the signing of the Edict of Milan in 311AD. The Edict was an edict of toleration that moved the early church into the age of compromise and opened of the doors of the church. Contemporary church movements have their history and practices rooted in the church of Pergamos, the church of Compromise, the beginning of the Roman Catholic Church; the word catholic simply means universal. From that point on, the church evolved and transitioned from one state to the next. Each transition of the church age built upon the issues of the previous church age.

The church of Pergamos gave rise to the church of Smyrna, characterized by the creation of monks and monasteries. The monks were those who opposed the church becoming a state church and separated themselves for sacred purposes. The monks saw the church being taken over by secularity and politics. They saw the pagan practices entering the sacred practices of the church as prescribed by Christ and the Apostles and desired to have no part of it! They developed a sacred order of clergy and catechetical teaching that prepared the clergy to represent the holy but not the unholy. Great men with brilliant biblical minds, such as St. Augustine and Martin Luther, were developed through the order of the monks. However, the monasteries eventually became a part of the Roman Catholic Church and embraced Roman Catholic theology.

The state church or the Imperial Church became more formalized and ritualistic in the church of Thyatira when the mystic practices of the Middle East became more and more prevalent and the Bible became less and less important. In fact, the priests preached in Latin and the people spoke another language. There was a total disconnect between the Bible, the pew, and the spiritual experience. While the church was highly liturgical, it was oxymoronic in its message. The word liturgy means the work of the people, yet, the priest was the sole laborer for God. He was the only one fit to be used by God because he vowed not to involve himself in the things of this world. Thus, he took vows of chastity and poverty to keep himself pure for God. Strands of that thought prevail today for all clergy but, of course, we know that those restrictions were unwise and unbiblical (1 Timothy 4:3). Modern-day results? Multi-million dollar law suits against the Roman Catholic Church, our modern day derivative of the Thyatira church, for the sexual abuse of young boys and girls by priests who were forced to choose between ministry and natural sexual urges for women. I'm not trying to be insensitive, but that's what happens when we compromise doctrine and do not adhere to the Word of God.

Pergamos opened the door and its practices were disseminated to the church of Thyatira and although the church of Sardis attempted reformation, the secularized culture was too embedded and its efforts failed, creating a double strand of the Protestant church. What do you mean double strand? Well, Sardis represents the Reformation movement that challenged the doctrine of Roman Catholicism, but eventually adopted a convenient modification of its practices that still did not represent the whole council of God. Having challenged the Roman Catholic Church, Sardis began a movement, the Reform tradition whose churches identified with the protest against Catholicism, yet still mirrored many of its practices, rituals, and formalism. Reformed churches exist today in the form of the Greek Orthodoxy, Lutheran, Presbyterian, Episcopalian denominations, among others. These churches flow out of the spirit of Sardis, which Christ called dead! As a whole, these churches don't have spiritual vibrancy nor do they empower their membership for the Great Commission Kingdom mission. I'm sure there are sincere people in Sardis churches but they have not totally separated themselves from the philosophies of this world. And though they are classified as Protestants, they are dead!

John mentions another church, situated between Sardis and Laodicea, and this is the second strand that I am referring to, the Missionary church. Historically, two strands of Protestantism have existed: the Reform church that is highly formal and reflects some of the practices of Roman Catholicism and the Church of Philadelphia or the Missionary church. The Missionary church serves as the foundation of Kingdom-minded churches that eventually emerged out of its movement. The Missionary church was responsible for attempting to preach the gospel through every open door of opportunity that God granted. It was and is a Great

Commission-based movement. This church was associated with the image of Christ holding the key of David (Kingdom analogy) (Revelation 3:7). This is the church that struggled to preach the Gospel abroad, for it had little strength, yet made every effort to keep His Word and honor His name and His will (Revelation 3:8). According to John, this church would eventually be in opposition with the compromised church of the Reform tradition. John refers to these churches as the synagogue of Satan, those who profess to have a covenant with Him but do not. This Missionary church has been promised, because of its faithfulness, to be kept from the hour of trial which is to come upon the whole world.

The church of Philadelphia is the church that eventually leads to the re-establishment of a Kingdom mentality in the entire church realm. Since this church is mentioned in light of the Rapture, or the great snatch, this church will simultaneously exist with the church of Laodicea. We know that the church of Philadelphia will give rise to churches that emphasize the Kingdom toward the end of the church age because Jesus said in Matthew 24:14:

> *And this gospel of the kingdom will be preached in all the world as a witness to all the nations, and then the end will come. (Matthew 24:14)*

Therefore, three branches of the church exist today: the Roman Catholic Church, the Reform church that birthed the church of Laodicea, and the Missionary church that evolves into the Kingdom church. This book focuses on rise of the Laodicean Church and Kingdom of God Church.

THE DOORS OF THE CHURCH ARE CLOSED

"And to the angel of the church of the Laodiceans write,

"'These things says the Amen, the Faithful and True Witness, the Beginning of the creation of God: "I know your works, that you are neither cold nor hot. I could wish you were cold or hot. So then, because you are lukewarm, and neither cold nor hot, I will vomit you out of My mouth. Because you say, 'I am rich, have become wealthy, and have need of nothing'— and do not know that you are wretched, miserable, poor, blind, and naked - I counsel you to buy from Me gold refined in the fire, that you may be rich; and white garments, that you may be clothed, that the shame of your nakedness may not be revealed; and anoint your eyes with eye salve, that you may see. As many as I love, I rebuke and chasten.

Therefore be zealous and repent. Behold, I stand at the door and knock. If anyone hears My voice and opens the door, I will come in to him and dine with him, and he with Me." (Revelation 3:14-20)

We are in the dispensation of the Laodicean church and the doors of the church are closed! When we examine Revelation 3:20, we are actually viewing a *dispensational change* because the church of Laodicea is the 7th and last church of Asia Minor. God is about to change how He deals with man. All things being equal, dispensationalism is not a new concept, thus when I state that the doors of the church are closed, I'm simply saying that this is the culture and context of the Laodicean church. Remember earlier, we stated that these were actual churches that had actual situations that were taking place during the times of John's writing. However, the seven churches of Asia Minor for many eschatologists represents the total church age. Thus, each church carries both an existential message and a futuristic or spiritual message that unfolds the mystery of the entire church age. The 7th church is the culmination of the entire church age and describes what the church will look like before the Rapture or the coming of the Lord in the clouds for His bride (1 Thessalonians 4:16-18).

Why do I say that? The first three chapters of Revelation establish Christ and His church; chapters two and three describe the seven churches of Asia Minor. The number seven in biblical numerology symbolizes completion, maturation, the end. Therefore, the seven churches unfold for us the events and activities that will take place throughout the church's entire existence, culminating with the church of Laodicea. When you examine statistics and the history of the contemporary Christian church, you will soon discover that the activities we see happening nationally and internationally in the church mirror the Church of Laodicea. The mentality of Laodicea cannot be reduced to that which reflects the church on the North American continent. I have had the privilege of preaching on multiple continents and establishing churches in North America, South Africa, West Africa, and Asia. I have seen the proof of the effects of the messages stated by the church of Laodicea. I have conducted leadership forums and seminars with international pastors who were extremely frustrated with this new watered down message that simply appeals to people's human nature and appetites while ignoring the will of God. The Laodicean movement is not simply in America, but has traveled world-wide. However, I must state for the record that the message was formed and disseminated on American soil.

The Laodicean message has created a consumer driven church market where people are no longer seeking God's will for their life; they are looking for the church that can meet their needs and give them good feelings. This consumerism refuses to promote any message of challenge and change; it is a message of affirmation not transformation. Because of the attitudes and actions of the Laodicean church, Christ is on the outside and only the devil knows who is on the inside. Why is Christ on the outside? Because the doors of the church are closed, even though all around the world, people are saying the doors of the church are open.

The last words spoken to the last church represent the fact that the church age was and will end. In the 4th chapter in Revelation, John speaks about being summonsed to 'come up here'. Evangelical Christianity agrees that the end of the church age culminates with the Rapture of the church. This is sometimes referred to as pre-Tribulation thought, which posits that the earth will experience seven years of macabre suffering and the Anti-Christ will come to power and rule for three and one-half years and then another dispensation will begin. (I apologize — I do not have time to delve deeply into this period of eschatology; however, please visit my website and order my series on the book of Revelation.) Before this seven year period begins, the church will be removed and the earth will no longer be preserved by the church (the salt of the earth).

We are living in what I consider to be the last days or the last dispensation of the church. In order to substantiate that we have entered the 7th church of Asia Minor era, the church's behavior must reflect the behavior described in Revelation 3. The seven churches reveal to us, along with other end time passages, that certain behaviors will be prevalent during this time that will delineate each unique dispensation or era of time. Someone may be thinking that this sounds so subjective and opinionated. "How can you say we're in the last days and the doors of the church are closed?" I'm not saying this without support. The Bible gives us signs of the end times, which gives us the ability to make prophetic statements. Studying what Paul, Peter, and Christ said in the New Testament about the signs of the end times, allows us to discern the times and seasons. In Matthew 24, Jesus, in His Olivet discourse gives us the signs of the end times. Paul writes to Timothy and gives us signs of the end times. Peter writes of the signs of the end times. The reason most folks don't know the signs of the times is because the signs of the times are in the Bible and the Bible is an irrelevant book to most Christians. Bible study is not promoted over the pulpit any longer. Paul speaks to Timothy and says, "The time will come when men will not endure sound doctrine" (2 Timothy 4:3). Beloved, that time has come!

People are no longer interested in learning the Bible and many contemporary preachers are not interested in preaching biblical doctrine. If you want to hide something from most Christians, put it in a Bible! Most Christians come to church without a Bible, but chastise their children for leaving their schoolbooks at home. What in the Father's name is wrong with us? We understand how important studying the law is to lawyers, studying medicine is to doctors, and drawing is to architects, but ignore how important knowing the scriptures is to being a believer or disciple of Christ. One American preacher, who has become a world icon in the church world, stated on a nationally syndicated talk show that he does not know doctrine nor does he desire to focus upon it. He stated that his ministry is to encourage people and that people don't want doctrine, they want answers on how to face everyday life. Wow! God gave Israel the Law to govern their lives and Jesus said that He came to fulfill it with His life as the Word of God. The Bible is the Word of God and should govern the believer's daily life. Without doctrine, we cannot live for Christ and we endanger the spiritual lives of others (1 Timothy 4:16). When you put doctrine out of the church, you have put Christ out of the church! Doctrine in the Greek simply means teaching. Teaching the fundamentals of the faith, while laying Christ as the chief cornerstone, is the foundation for Christian living.

Jesus spoke very little about the church, but He mainly spoke about the Kingdom of God. The church holds the keys to the Kingdom, yet many people come to church but have not entered or seen the Kingdom of God. Jesus did not come upon the earth to give you an invitation to the church. He came to invite you to the Kingdom. So if you are just 'going to church' and that's all you know, you are living for the wrong institution. The church age eventually ends with two things:

1. The rise of the Laodicean church - characterized by its message of rich and increase and have need of nothing; and,
2. The preaching of the gospel of the Kingdom – after which the end shall occur.

When we consider dispensational thought, which makes a distinction between Israel and the church, (which I support wholeheartedly), the prophetic significance of the church is extremely crucial during our life time. The Middle East is a ticking time bomb. No one knows exactly what is going to happen, except we know that at some point the Jewish Temple will be rebuilt and the battle over the Dome of the Rock, the worship place for both Muslims and Jews and the original site of the Jewish temple, will escalate. What you have to understand is that before that time bomb goes off, America must not be a factor. Most mainstream preachers are not going to say that because they have bought into the politics of this country. The only one that can say that is a free thinking man that speaks by the Spirit of God, not as a gloom and doom preacher, but as one who understands the scriptures.

The United States has pledged allegiance to Israel and we are Israel's big brother — we're closely connected to them politically and economically. I am not trying to make any kind of moral or spiritual statement about this relationship; I'm simply stating reality. Therefore, we must protect our interests. Everybody knows that he that touches Israel touches America and so Israel's enemies will only go so far with her, but terrorism against America is increasing as evidenced by 9/11. Despite popular opinion, our nation has been involved in some business affairs with Israel that others have not viewed favorably. Israel is hated by all of its surrounding neighbors and they have a desire to destroy Israel, but one of the things that is stopping them is the commitment and the covenant between Israel and America, and of course, the prophetic clock.

Almost all biblical scholars agree that America is not mentioned in eschatology. I know we think it's a great country and personally, I wouldn't want to live in any other place but America. However, I'm a citizen of two kingdoms. I'm a citizen of the Kingdom of God and America. And, even though I wouldn't want to live any place else but America, my love for the United States does not stop me from seeing what's happening in this country. My patriotism doesn't blind me from the fact that regardless of how many Americans think America is the New Israel, America, the most powerful nation in the world, is eventually going to fall. When the World Trade Center was bombed, every American citizen became afraid for his life. For the first time, terrorism affected us on our own soil and the attack exposed our weaknesses.

Folks were scared to go to church, sporting events, and even the mall. We all wanted to know — "Where is the next place they're going to hit? What if they hit this place? What if they hit that place?" People were scared. The next thing you know, the anthrax threat began and people didn't want to pick up their mail. Listen, you know you're scared when you don't even want to open up your mail that can potentially have money inside. You know people want to take you out when technology has become so sophisticated that terrorists figured out a way to make liquid bombs with detonators on board a plane and inside shoes! These terrorists could care less about how you feel about what America has done - they just want to take out Americans. With America unmentioned in eschatology, we must be aware of all threats against this nation as signs of the times.

Just like we thought we were safe in America before 9/11, oblivious to rising terrorism in the world, many people feel safe in the church, oblivious to the obvious warnings in scripture about the end times. No matter how redundant and clichéd this may sound, we truly are living in the end times and the doors of the church are closed. The true church will be raptured and another will be left. The only way to secure your eternal future is by receiving the message of the Kingdom of God that exalts Christ, not simply as Savior but also Lord and King! We can no longer afford to operate in the foolishness of a secularized church that is ignorant of God's Word and His Kingdom.

So, you've got to know where you are on the prophetic clock of God. The world was not created to exist indefinitely.

Everything we see is evolving to a climax. It is coming to a pinnacle of experience and then our entire world of existence will come to a climatic end. The only way that you can determine where we are on the prophetic clock of God or the timetable of God is to pay attention to the signs of the times. We know from Ecclesiastes 3 that there is a time and a season for everything under the sun. Everything must run its course on the prophetic time clock of our Sovereign Lord. Indeed, even David said to God, "My times are in your hand." (Psalms 31:15). It is an eschatological reality due to the inevitability of scripture that the doors of the church must close and remain closed. So it does not matter what preacher gets up and states the traditional statement, "The doors of the church are open — will there be one, by letter, baptism, or Christian experience?"…the doors of the church are closed! Individuals must invite Him in for relationship and He promises that whoever overcomes the closed doors, he will sit with Him and the Father in heaven.

Even though the doors are closed, thankfully, Christ is still knocking. Please listen for His voice and wake up before it is too late and you are left trying to hear God in the midst of the Tribulation period! I know that it is extremely difficult to hear the voice of God in the midst of a compromised church. This is the reason why you must learn and study the scriptures to show yourself approved. (2 Timothy 2:15).

Many people find it difficult to recognize the present voice of God because they have been mis-taught by the church with doctrine tarnished by the selfish agendas of the power class, the ignorance of the clergy class, and the appetites of a social class. Many people are asking "What should I believe? Because a lot of what has me bound, I learned in the church! The church is supposed to be 'the house of God, the church of the Living God, the pillar and ground of the truth!'" (1 Timothy 3:15).

My position concerning the day and time we live is that humanity is in the final stage of our understanding of God. As stated earlier, this is the dispensation of the church age or the dispensation of grace, but within the church age, our understanding of God has progressed dispensationally in thought as well. Again, the doors of the church are closed because of two reasons: the rise of the church of Laodicea and the preaching of the gospel of the Kingdom of God. The Bible prophesied about the gospel of the Kingdom being preached in Matthew 24:14 but until this century, most churches lacked the understanding and exposure to the concept. But we know that the doors of the church are closed because of the emergence of 'Kingdom teaching' in some churches. Even though men and women of God in academia have known and written about the Kingdom of God, instruction in Kingdom doctrine has only occurred in churches recently. According to the prophetic clock of God, the time is now!

Looking at the church historically from a doctrinal perspective, I want to consider the concept of dispensation from a doctrinal perspective in order to again examine how the church doors are closed. For this cause, I have developed Seven Dispensations of Theological Renewal that parallel the progression of the church age:

1. Revelation
2. Identification
3. Salvation
4. Regeneration
5. Impartation
6. Participation
7. Exaltation

With this in mind I want to begin by looking at these seven epochs of time and examine the church's teachings.

The Dispensation of Revelation. The early church was given the most comprehensive understanding of the Gospel of the Kingdom and the mission of Christ. The early church gleaned from eyewitnesses, the disciples, on the proper way to live for Christ. The disciples were extremely important in ensuring that the message that they had heard and seen was spread throughout the world. The disciples were not operating out of hearsay; they were actual eyewitnesses who experienced the ministry of Jesus first hand and who were trained by Jesus Himself (Acts 4:20). The early church not only benefited from the teaching of the disciples but also the Gentiles; the disciples presided on the Jerusalem Council concerning the integration of the Gentiles. The early church represented the most powerful representation of the call and cause of Christ that we know. The gospels give us detailed narratives of the life, mission, and teachings of Christ, as witnessed by His disciples. The book of Acts demonstrates for us how the disciples (later the Apostles) executed what Christ commissioned them to do for His Kingdom. Thus, the gospels and the book of Acts serve as a historical record of the intended focus and scope of the mission of the church and its teachings.

I refer to this era as the Dispensation of Revelation because this is the era in which the Holy Spirit inspired men to write the Word of God. I want to make sure I emphasize the preeminence I give to the Word of God. The Bible is not given to us by interpretation, thus, it has no errors; men, assigned to provide the world with the Word of God, penned the Bible through God-breathed inspiration. If anyone or any era contained a holistic understanding of the Word of God, it was the 1st century saints and the early church. The early church was the first and only dispensation in which the mind of God was understood concerning His Kingdom, the church, and the world. The time span for the early church occurred from Pentecost through the 3rd century. This church actually laid the foundation for the gospel to be preached upon every continent. This church witnessed to excellencies of Christ from Jerusalem to the uttermost parts of the world! Its members understood their mission, their methodology, their mandate, and their message! The early church was persecuted for its faith, dispersed, and its leaders became martyrs for the faith.

The Dispensation of Identification. This dispensation was both a blessing and a cursing. This dispensation was birthed in the 4th century upon the cessation of Christian persecution with the signing of the Edict of Milan. This official document ended Christian persecution and allowed Christians to freely practice their faith. During this era, Christianity became the official religion of the Roman Empire. That's right — to be a Roman citizen was to be a Christian and to be a Christian was to be a Roman citizen. To be Roman and Christian was synonymous in nomenclature. With the freedom to practice Christianity, void of the fear and threat of persecution and death, the church could now attend to its unfinished business. However, since Christianity became the official religion of Rome, there was no need for the church to fulfill the Great Commission. The entire Roman Empire was automatically Christian and baptized as infants into the faith.

This era opened doors of the church! The Roman Empire, led by the influence of Constantine the Great, opened the doors of the church and everyone became a member. Conversion was unnecessary in this new Christian religion as long as you were a citizen or member of the Roman Empire. The empire thought that one of the highest privileges the church could have ever been given was Roman legitimacy. The Roman Empire was believed to be one of the most advanced and superior empires in the world. This marriage between the state and the church would haunt the Christian church forever!

The blessing that came out this era was the peace and tranquility the church experienced that allowed the collection of all the writings of the apostles. Those men, inspired to compile, copy, and translate the Bible, gathered in 397 AD at the council of Carthage. Prior to collecting all of the writings, this era was famously known for its church doctrine councils. These councils were designed to decide what would be the official doctrines of Christianity. These councils would convene and rigorously argue and debate scripture and theological themes. Many of the most renowned theological thinkers, commonly referred to as the patristics or early church fathers, emerged from these councils. Many of them, originating from Northern Africa, became known for developing the primary doctrines of the church formally named church creeds. Some of the most important creeds that came out of these councils were: the Nicene Creed, the Constantinople Creed, the Athanasian Creed, and the Apostle's Creed. Also among these councils were Chalcedon and Ephesus, who were very instrumental during the Dispensation of Identification.

Why do I refer this era as the dispensation of identification? The Dispensation of Identification allowed the church to fully identify who Christ was in relationship to God the Father and God the Holy Spirit. During this era, Christ was declared, *homousia,* or of the same substance as God. After careful study of the scriptures, Christ was declared fully God and fully man, while not confounding or mixing the two natures of Christ. This is the dispensation wherein we identified who God was in relationship to His triune presentation — One God in Three Persons. Our present-day understanding of Christ as both Lord and Savior and God and man developed during this era. This era was marked by such great thinkers as Athanasius, St. Augustine, Origen, Tertullian, Chrysostom, Cyprian, the three Cappadocians, and others. This era extended from the 4th century through the 16th century. Consider this: for the first 16 centuries minus the early church, the only revelation the church had was the identity of God.

The Dispensation of Salvation. This era, beginning in the 1500's, is called the pre-Reformation movement. During this period, the theology of the Roman Catholic Church was beginning to be challenged by men such as John Wycliffe and John Huss. The Reformation period culminated under the efforts of Martin Luther who had an experience that caused him to re-examine the scriptures concerning what the church taught about eternal life and how one obtains eternal life. Luther disagreed with the extra measures the church required people to perform in order to be in right standing with God and please Him (works righteousness). Luther's research led him to conclude that salvation cannot be granted by the Roman Catholic Church or through penance or prayers for the dead. Luther concluded that the only way one could have eternal life was through four Latin phrases: solo fide, solo gratia, sola scriptura, and sola Christos (by faith alone, by grace alone, by scripture alone, and by Christ alone is a man saved). Luther challenged Roman Catholic scholars to an open theological debate concerning salvation by nailing his 95 theses or statements against the theology of the Roman Catholic Church on the door of Wittenberg. His theses condemned their teachings. Of course that did not go over very well and Luther never got a chance to debate his positions, but had to be hurried out of the city and placed in hiding. Luther was a wanted man for concluding that you did not need to embrace the traditions of the Roman Catholic Church in order to have a relationship with Christ. He stated that in order to be saved or have a relationship with God, only faith, grace, scripture, and Christ were required. Luther was not attempting to shut the doors of the Roman Catholic Church; he was simply challenging the church to rethink its teaching.

The reason I refer to this dispensation as the dispensation of Salvation is because Luther's treatises serve as the basis for our soteriology or doctrine of salvation. Luther was not a lone ranger in this endeavor — men such as John Calvin and Ulrich Zwingli also challenged Roman Catholicism and its lack of biblical basis for its beliefs and practices. The Dispensation of Salvation covered the 1500's and the 1600's. Wow! Consider this — we are in the 1600's and the only thing we know about God is who He is and the requirements of salvation.

The Dispensation of Regeneration. This dispensation has its roots in the English Reformation. The study of English Protestantism and Roman Catholicism is a very interesting historical investigation for those of you who enjoy soap operas. The official religion of England depended upon what king or queen was in office. The changing of the guards was always accompanied with drama. However, one of the greatest reformers and preachers who ever lived came out of this era in the 1700's, a man by the name of John Wesley. Wesley was a tremendous preacher who has been called the father of the Methodist church. He was an itinerant preacher who traveled around the country preaching the gospel. He could have been what some would refer to as a fire and brimstone preacher. His message focused upon regeneration; he was instrumental in re-instituting the message of regeneration in the church. He boldly proclaimed "You must be born again"!

He and his brother Charles Wesley, along with other powerful English preachers, were instrumental in heralding the message of regeneration for two centuries. John and Charles Wesley, George Whitefield, and others were also instrumental in influencing religious groups, like the Quakers and the Puritans, toward religious pietism. Wesley focused upon ensuring that people had the internal witness of the Spirit of God to confirm that they were a child of God. I refer to this as the Dispensation of Regeneration because the message of conversion was preached and embraced in the 18th and 19th century. Wesley stressed the spiritual experience; he saw the need for believers to have two encounters with God, salvation and perfect love, because both were acts of grace. Wesley's fervor earned him title of the primary founder of the 'you-must-be-born-again' movement. This is also referred to as the Great Awakening or the revivalist era [Jonathan Edwards, George Whitefield, John and Charles Wesley, D.L. Moody, Charles Spurgeon, etc in England, Scotland, and America] In America, the Great Awakening period produced the message of rejuvenation and gave birth to the first black Baptist church in mid-18th century America — Silver Bluff Baptist Church of Aiken County, South Carolina.

Let's review for a moment: here we are in the 1700's to the 1900's and the only thing that we have regained and recaptured from the early church so far is: who God is, how one is saved, and in order to be saved, you must be born again. As you can see, one of the reasons the church is crippled and its members are ignorant and trapped inside is due to its need for theological renewal. We left the doctrine of the early church and have been poisoned through the opened doors of the church that have allowed everything in and out!

The Dispensation of Impartation. This is the dispensation of what has been called the Baptism in the Holy Sprit, evidenced by glossolalic speech, or "tongues". This dispensation was an extremely important dispensation marked by the number five, which is the number of grace. This dispensation gave birth to the re-visitation of the Holy Spirit. While this dispensation probably represents one of the most controversial dispensations within the Protestant movement, it served as the catalyst for worldwide ministry. The Baptism in the Holy Spirit was the dispensation in which the Spirit came to help us unify and empower God's people for service.

However, due to racism in America and the lack of sound biblical doctrine, the movement was minimized in America while having worldwide affects abroad. This movement took place during a time when one of the most heretical, theological works (although heralded as one of the most scholarly works of the ages) was published: "The Negro: A Beast or in the Image of God" by Professor C. Carroll. His work was launched as a scientific and theological project that would educate Americans about the place of Negros in America. He stated that blacks belong to the animal kingdom of beasts and were created on the fifth day. He said that Negroes were pre-Adamites.

At the same time, God sent an over-abundance of His Spirit to a group of people worshipping on Azusa St. in California. The Holy Spirit ignited His people for ministry, but to no avail. Racism and hatred were too prominent for whites to identify with blacks, even in church. Society deemed the entire movement heretical. The main reason the movement was highly rejected was because its leader was a one-eyed black man named William J. Seymour. Seymour received the teaching for this experience from a white gentleman by the name of William Parham. Historians suggest that Parham, who was a KKK sympathizer, never experienced glossolalic speech. The Holy Spirit was first believed to have fallen upon one of Parham's students, Agnes Ozman. After reports of the Holy Spirit falling upon the house church in which Seymour pastored spread, the movement began to catch the attention of the world.

The Holy Spirit fell heavy upon those services and people not only spoke in other tongues, but other manifestations occurred on Bonnie Brea St. The movement later spread to Azusa St. and, as the young people say, it was off the chain. People were experiencing the Baptism of the Holy Spirit for the empowerment of service and the unification of God's people. Unfortunately, the movement did not unite

God's people but further divided them along the lines of race and class. The movement slowly began to be identified with the rigidity of the holiness movement and the classism of the Assemblies of God.

This movement was pivotal and continues today as the most vital and vibrant aspect of the Body of Christ. Today, this experience has crossed denominational lines, racial lines, and geographical lines. The Baptism in the Holy Spirit is a global movement of the Spirit. The normative experience of speaking in other tongues in the early church was not known in our contemporary context until the 1800's in Great Britain under the leadership of Edward Irving and the Catholic Apostolic Church of Scotland and then later, the United States on Azusa St. Beloved, it took us until the 20th century to come to know the following: who God is, how is one saved, you must be born again, and how one is empowered for service. In the fifth Dispensation of Impartation, we learned the necessity of the power of the Holy Spirit for Christian service.

The Dispensation of Participation. This era covers what has been called the Pentecostal/Charismatic/Full Gospel movements. These movements have been instrumental in laying the foundation for layman engaging in their faith and participating in worship. This movement gave birth to prayer ministries, such as "Can ye not tarry for one hour?" by Dr. Larry Lea. This dispensation gave rise to an emphasis on studying the scriptures and trusting God according to His Word. During this era, teachings on spiritual warfare and seed sowing for ministry began. This dispensation is responsible for the Praise and Worship movement that created a new genre of interactive music, praise dancing, and the integration of the fine arts in worship.

Six, in biblical numerology, is the number of man. The 6th dispensation of theological renewal was the dispensation wherein man was now an active participant in worship. This aspect of the church was something totally different from Catholicism and the mainline churches and revolutionary in the European church world. The 6th dispensation was the era in which men were allowed to express their faith and the formality of religion was subtly abandoned. The need for formally trained clergy diminished and an emphasis on Bible training was traded for experience. This is the era when people stopped saying 'the Bible states' and exchanged biblical authority for spiritual experience. The new statements are 'the Spirit said to me' and 'the Holy Ghost taught me'. Laymen no longer demanded that their leaders be trained in the Word, and denominations, who demanded trained leaders, declined. So this dispensation has produced a generation of ignorant pulpits: men and women, who taught simply from inspiration, totally devoid of information through education. This era became not only a dispensation wherein man engaged his faith, but he also went to extremes, to the point of no biblical accountability and a subsequent rise in pride/ insecurity, arrogance, and spiritual deception due to a lack of a firm theological education. This is the era in which the blind began to lead the blind. Please don't get me wrong: everyone does not have to go to seminary, but everyone, who is called to pastor or preach, must sit under someone who has been trained at some level in properly interpreting the Word of God. Even Paul, who knew the Law, trained under Gamalial after his conversion and call before he began his ministry for Christ.

Let's re-cap the dispensations before we go to what I call the last dispensation of theological renewal:

1. Revelation: The Early Church (Comprehensive understanding of the Mission, Mandate, Methodology and the Message of Christ and His Kingdom)

2. Identification: The Roman Empire/Imperial Church (Who is Christ in relationship to the Triune God and man)
3. Salvation: The Reformation (How is one saved)
4. Regeneration: The Great Awakening (You must be born again)
5. Impartation: The Azusa Outpouring (Empowerment for service and unity)
6. Participation: The Pentecostal/Charismatic/Full Gospel movement (Engaging one's faith at every level)

The Dispensation of Exaltation. This is the Dispensation of the Kingdom of God. When you review how long it has taken us to re-capture what the 1st century knew and practiced, it is simply amazing. From the 4th century to the 21st century believers were finally challenged to focus upon the proclamation, explanation, and demonstration of the Kingdom of God — the things Christ focused upon when He was here. This is the dispensation wherein truly Spirit-filled people will abandon the banner of traditionalism and church, which is rooted in the sociological whims of a racist, classist, and heretical church. Even though the Bible is referenced, the basis for its beliefs and teachings of the sociological church are not biblical. Christ has a people that will come out from those who have a form of godliness but deny the power – the Church of Laodicea. Paul admonishes Timothy to stay away from them (2 Timothy 3:5). There are people who have learned to enjoy church without Christ and they have been doing it so long, they no longer have the ability to recognize that He is no longer present in the building.

Through a process, the church of Laodicea put Christ out of the church. The process involved the following:

- The exaltation of culture
- The exaltation of class
- The exaltation of cause

When the church placed cultural preferences above Kingdom culture, the church invited Christ to exit. After that, the church categorized people according to their class, thus asking for the Christ-founded egalitarian scale (how you measure someone's value) to be abandoned. The church further exemplified the lack of the need for the affirmation of Christ. Then, the last thing that finally put Him out was when the church rallied its own causes, and not the cause of Christ. Thus, the Great Commission was exchanged for financial commissions and personal commission (a better you).

The 7th dispensation will focus upon the proclamation of the Kingdom of God as a witness and then the end of the church age. Its mission is to bring people to Christ and His Kingdom and invite people out of the closed doors of the church. In this dispensation, the church will learn more about the Kingdom and walk in Kingdom power and authority, literally snatching souls out of the snares of the enemy. This is also an era in which you must be careful because men have already begun changing the Kingdom message to lift the authority of man and not God. In the Kingdom, God is Sovereign and we are His faithful servants. His Kingdom does not reflect a British or Chinese kingdom; His Kingdom is a biblical Kingdom wherein He alone sits on the throne as the One True King. Be careful when men tell you the King has to get your permission to act.

In God's Kingdom, His subjects die daily to their flesh and live daily for His Kingdom. This is the opposite of what the church of Laodicea is characterized for; their testimony is, "We are rich in increase, have become wealthy, and have need of nothing!" If you notice, this church is a church that focuses upon its confession of wealth, for the text states "For you say!" It is a church that seeks after riches and material gain. It is a church that prioritizes increase. You cannot listen to Christian TV without hearing one of those three Laodicean messages: 1) watch your confession, 2) you are called to be a millionaire thus make a switch to rich, and 3) by the covenant of Abraham, expect an increase. Now don't get me wrong — who doesn't desire to have his needs taken care of in abundance? The problem is not money - it is focus! Subscription to this philosophy means believing God for material things while ignoring the salvation of thousands daily. The Bible states that God added to the church daily. I wonder how many souls are ignored while men seek increase.

Beloved, we must listen attentively for the voice of God as revealed in His Word. As mentioned earlier, it is very difficult to decipher between the Word of God and the traditions of men because when the doors of the church were opened by Constantine and widened by the church of England and the American church system, all kinds of things came in. A lot of what came in the church was taught as the revelation of God but was nothing more than the culture of men.

The Laodicean Church: A Church without Jesus

I've got an important newsflash! The sociological church that was opened by Constantine, continued by the Pope, granted power by the kings, and used as a mechanism of control by American presidents, is now closed. The counterfeit church – the sociological church – is the Church of Laodicea. The Laodicean church was the lukewarm church who said that they are rich, wealthy, and have need of nothing. Satan has perpetrated the ultimate deception in mass scale, where, in true Alice in Wonderland-like fashion, 'up' is 'down' and 'down' is 'up'. The American church, in its current state, is a gathering of Laodicea. It is during this era that the church has effectively kicked Christ out, boasting of its prosperity and its lack of dependency upon Him (Revelation 3:17).

As discussed earlier, God frames the first three chapters of Revelation as the church age. This age depicts the behavior of the entire church age and then leads us into what is referred to by many as the Rapture. Hence, in Ephesians when Christ says He is coming back, that scripture is referring to the Rapture. When He comes back, He comes back in the era called the Laodicean era. The Laodicean era then ushers the church into the Rapture. Thus, the Laodicean era is the last era of the church; it is the church in eschatology. The Laodicean church is the church under compromise that has locked Christ out and has become self sufficient.

The church of Philadelphia represents those who are on the outside with Christ the King. Those on the inside represent 21st century prosperity Christians that are enterprising and industrious, with vestiges of the dead church of Sardis. But Jesus describes them as wretched, pitiful, poor, blind, and naked. Due to the Laodicea's political and money emphasis, our text says the doors of the church are closed, and Jesus is standing outside the door trying to get in. Now Jesus said it's 'My church' and hence when it's 'His church,' you should never find Him on the outside knocking on *His* door trying to get in. But He is!

Isn't that ironic? Jesus, on the outside of His own church, looking in: "Behold, I stand at the door and knock. If anyone hears My voice and opens the door, I will come in to him and dine with him, and he with Me." (Revelation 3:20) Since He is knocking, Jesus refuses to force His way in. The doors being closed also signifies that Jesus is no longer welcome in the church corporately. I am fond of saying that God is a "gentleman God," which means that Jesus will not force His way through the door any more than God would have forced Adam's obedience in the Garden. We refer to this in theology as free moral agency. Jesus will stand outside and make His appeal to individuals who hear His voice. He requires an invitation before He will enter the hearts of those who could or would respond to His voice.

Christ on the outside implies that the Word of God is no longer the foundation of the church; the Word of God is no longer directing the affairs of the contemporary church. The Word of God is not being used to discover the will of God; it is being exploited and misappropriated to accumulate wealth or so called blessings or covenant rights. Notice that Jesus, however, did not say listen for my voice but He emphasized hearing – hearing to the point of obedience. Listening and hearing...I'm sure you want to know the difference. The difference can be observed between the response of a child when you call and the response of an adult. When we call an adult, they may or may not respond based on their interests and time constraints. When we call a child, we expect immediate action – that is the response Jesus expected. Jesus asked us to open the doors of our hearts for Him, but unfortunately, He has been voted out of the church and now is on the outside, knocking because He can't get in.

This is a very perplexing scenario, especially when we consider that the church is Christ's creation and His possession! He died a horrid and excruciating death for His Bride and is responsible for its growth. He promised to come back again for the church and escort the church to glory (Ephesians 5:27). What I find most significant is that you see Christ standing at the door knocking and requesting *personal entrance*, not corporate entrance. He is not asking to come inside the entire gathering. He will only come in by individual invitation to dine with those who desire to dine with Him. As we read this text in its context, we discover that Christ is speaking to the church; however, the contemporary church uses this verse to invite people to Christ and church membership. Don't you find it interesting that this was Christ's invitation to the church to return back to Him and the church totally ignores the context and refers to it as a sinner's altar call? This text does not show us an invitation for the sinner to come to know Christ, His cross, and His crucifixion, but this is a call to recognize His voice; it is the plea of God to a wayward church.

We previously examined the historical context of what led to the doors of the church being opened, and we attempted to answer the questions: Who was the architect? Who was the locksmith? Who passed out the keys to *those doors* when the Bible tells us that Christ gave us the keys to the Kingdom? He said nothing about giving us keys to the doors of the church. Nevertheless, we have a church that has created another paradigm for its existence and a new process for inclusion.

When we consider Christ's original plans for His church and what the church ultimately evolves into during the Laodicean age, we must ask ourselves, "How could it get that way if it was His church?" This is a critical question because if Christ was the progenitor of the church, the church should carry His DNA. The church should actually reflect Him since she is His offspring. However, the church of Laodicea doesn't look anything like Christ, which is a serious issue. There is an old cliché that goes something like this: 'momma's baby, daddy's maybe'. When your offspring doesn't resemble you, you, as the seed giver, must question the legitimacy of the genetics. In essence, there is a possibility that someone else has been dipping in the cookie jar.

I teach discipleship from a cell cycle approach examining the three phase process of producing life. I examine the interphase, mitosis, and cytokinesis as the model for producing offspring. What's the point? The point is every cell carries the DNA of the parent cell and resembles the parent cell. Therefore, the church is the offspring of Christ and should reflect His DNA or God's agenda, which is the agenda of His father. The church that Christ has been put out of or has found no more use for does not reflect His DNA. We know the author of all evil is Satan – an enemy has done this – even to the church of the Lord Jesus Christ. He infiltrated the church in order to cause mankind to stray from God. Jesus referred to the church as His bride, however, when the church 'married' the state during the Church of Pergamos, a counterfeit church was produced, the Church of Laodicea.

What's so sad, beloved, is that Satan is very masterful in what he does. He created a church full of spiritual and theological illiterates who are insensitive to and unconcerned about the will of their Master. Theologically, in the average church, you can preach on a kindergarten level because all the congregants want to do is hear a few songs, a supporting nursery rhyme, and receive a "positive and affirming" word. The average Christian is not concerned about Bible doctrine, when the Bible teaches that doctrine is the safeguard against heresies and deception. Doctrine is what saves both you and others (Ephesians 4:14; 1 Timothy 4:16)

There are two strands of churches in society today. One is the church of culture, dominated by the "isms": racism, classism, sexism, denominationalism, and doctrinal eroticism. This church is referred to as the "worldly church" by H. Richard Niebuhr in his work "The Kingdom of God in America." The worldly church is a church that seeks to maintain the old order in society and with it, the power of the aristocrats, owners of property, and others with vested rights. In times past, folks with those interests would be termed "the MAN" or the "the powers that be." Niebuhr wrote: "We want a God without wrath who took a man without sin born into a Kingdom without justice through ministrations of a Christ without a cross."[19]

In other words, Niebuhr says we want everything on our own terms. Theologians and great pulpiteers have attempted in a minuscule way to challenge the contemporary church and its marriage to culture vs. its commitment to Christ. The church of Christ has been given specific orders concerning its mission as the embassy of the Kingdom. However, culture has redefined the church as an institution rather than as a living organism that reflects Christ's Kingdom. So, people see the church as merely existing to provide aid and relief. People think that the church is the place you are supposed to come when you're down and out and get whatever you need.

Niebuhr, in the 1940s, also wrote about the danger of the church politicizing itself and of politicians usurping the Christian church and using it for their own desires rather than the church being used to further the desires of Christ the King. He wrote that the worldly church engages in a sort of irresponsible, perversion of Christian social responsibility that results from the substitution of God's approval for society's approval. The question in the mind of the church, which has fallen into this temptation, is "what does the nation or the civilization require?" The church thinks of itself as responsible to the society for God, rather than to God for society. In this situation, the church is more concerned about social approval and disapproval than about divine judgment. Its end is to promote the glory of society rather than its God-ordained role and the glory of God.

H. Richard Niebuhr notes the following regarding the temptation to worldliness:

"However, the temptation to worldliness arises also when a radical or a revolutionary group seeks to seize power and when a church undertakes to gain the approval of such a group. The former temptation is great because of the church's interest in order; the latter because of its interest in the reformation of unjust order, but in either case if it seeks to gain the good even if it was simply for society or parts of society and makes itself responsible to them for supplying certain religious value, it has become irresponsible as a Christian since it has substituted men for God."[17]

What I believe Niebuhr was saying is that the church is often called on by secular society to provide the values and rules needed to under gird its causes. A case in point is gambling. Nowhere in Scripture do we find laws against gambling, but secular America needed the prohibition of gambling to be a Christian virtue because so much money was being made through underground black market gambling and the government was losing money in potential tax revenue. As a result, secular society had to prevail upon the conscience of people and used the church to make gambling a moral issue when the only reference in scripture to "gambling" is when the Roman soldiers at the cross gambled for the garment of Christ. Other than that, there is no scripture against gambling. [However, we may rightly say that it is bad stewardship or that it is an inappropriate way to seek gain. On the other hand, investments are gambling so is this improper?] Please don't get me wrong. I am not saying I encourage gambling or believe that the state lottery is a godly opportunity or you should gamble as a believer. I'm simply saying that sometimes the church is being used as the world's vassal or pawn unaware.

Laodicean Trap #1: Cultural Acceptance

This strand of the church has allowed itself to be used historically by a society and culture that once upon a time really desired to have a form of godliness. However, this same society has progressed in liberalism and resents biblical values that conflict with human desire. This society has chosen to embrace an ethereal spirituality that is rooted in self-centeredness and situational ethics that are totally subjective. The church has attempted to maintain relevance and survival in a godless society by providing cultural and racial identity rather than Kingdom identity, reinforced by misinterpreted scripture. This church is trying to re-position itself to be accepted by society and to find usefulness in a context that no longer respects nor appreciates the Bible.

Thus, this church has emerged as the motivational church that encourages the human spirit rather than preaching the message of transformation through repentance and embracing the gospel of the kingdom. It is a church that has lost its saltiness and is now being trampled under the feet of men (Matthew 5:13). This strand offers a mass appeal of self-help and encouragement through positive feel-good messages. Please understand I am not suggesting that the gospel, which means good news, does not make us feel good. However, the good news becomes good only after the bad news, which is, without Christ, I am condemned. The good news is that He became my substitute and paid the price for my sin. Yet, in order to embrace the gospel, I must repent or change my entire mentality concerning life and its application. I must become a new creation, I must be born again! (John 3:3-5)

Laodicean Trap #2: Money

The message of the sociological church is "I am rich in increase, have become wealthy, and have need of nothing" (Revelation 3:17). The mechanism that allows the Laodicean church to declare that about itself is money. Their skewed prosperity message permeates millions of churches world-wide. When Paul wrote Gaius in 3 John 2, he prayed that Gaius would prosper or be successful on his journey to fulfill the will of God. Prosperity has been reduced to money and personal wealth. The ministers of these churches make well known how well they are doing based on the 'so-called' application of God's Word. Prosperity has become the measuring rod for a believer's faithfulness, piety, and commitment to the things of God. Yet, we have very devout Christians that live in 3rd World countries. If wealth is the measure of one's faith and the Bible instructs us on gaining wealth, why doesn't this new gospel apply to them?

The Laodicean church has sold out to the god of mammon, but mammon brings with it all kinds of evil according to 1 Timothy 6:10. Paul said the love of money is the root of all kinds of evil. Satan uses our love of money to create pipe dreams that don't tell the whole story. Case in point: Judas had an agenda in which he contrived a scheme to force Christ into inaugurating His Kingdom right now. He saw the benefits of betraying Christ compared to 30 pieces of silver. In his pipe dream, he probably thought about all the particular ways he was going to spend his 30 pieces of silver. He probably saw himself with his 30 pieces of silver, buying himself a brand new set of nets because they had holes. He probably saw himself getting some fresh garments and treating himself to some gourmet food, not to mention when he coupled the silver with the money he was already stealing out the treasury, he probably saw himself faring very well. One of the things that Judas did not know was that guilt came with the money, and with the money came unexpected things like Christ not inaugurating His Kingdom in the natural as he desired. So what did Judas do with his 30 pieces of silver? He threw it on the ground and tried to give it back because his love of money came with all kinds of evils.

This same spirit exists in the church of Laodicea and has sold Christ out for mammon, things they trust in for survival. Christian TV has become increasingly difficult to watch if you desire some type of spiritual impartation. Don't get me wrong — there are some ministries that do a wonderful job but they are few, comparatively speaking. Pretty much, Christian broadcasting, the particular network does not matter, shows the same line up, talking about increase, prosperity, abundance, and blessings. The religious broadcasters form what appears to be a monopoly on the Christian airways. The stations help to make them very popular and in turn, they pay the station a nice rate. The Bible states that Satan is the prince of the air(ways). He is controlling the church's message through broadcasting that promotes Laodicean principles of wealth and increase.

In Matthew 6:24, Jesus explains the potential dichotomy of man's worship in the Kingdom Constitution; I am referring to what has been traditionally called the Sermon on the Mount as the Kingdom Constitution. Matthew 5 begins with the Beatitudes as the Preamble to the constitution. Jesus states, "No man can serve two masters. You either love one or hate the other. No man can serve both God and mammon." Now we've become extremely intellectual, and we know how to rephrase anything we want to rephrase. So no money worshipper will *say* they worship money. Most of the folks that are worshipping money simply believe they are 'taking care of their families', trying to live the prosperous life, or simply 'trying to leave their children's children an inheritance.' In the church, people must be aware that the enemy to spiritual progress will be their economic progress.

It is a sad reality that many who could have been a part of the remnant church that preaches the Kingdom will find themselves hanging out in Laodicea with all of the 'so-called faith preachers', saying 'money preachers.' If you don't watch yourself, you will be hanging out with all of those that are spending exorbitant amounts of money trying to be recognized for 'making it' and success. There are 'men of God' who challenge their partners to give millions of dollars for ministry that never reach out to the lost or open the gates of the Kingdom of God. We have not been given the keys to financial freedom — we have been given the keys to the Kingdom! Many people are taken advantage of by hook and crook preachers who prophesy for money. Others are taken advantage by televangelists who raise money through TV, promising that if you sow a seed, God is going to perform a miracle. While miracles are most definitely one manifestation of the Kingdom, God never ever gave us a methodology for ministry that involves receiving money simply to take care of our living expenses. It is exploitation! Many of the people that are sending monies into these ministries are blue collar, lower class workers that don't know how to get out of the financial bind that they are in. Jesus commanded us to seek the Kingdom of God first and all other things would be added to us. (Matthew 6:33)

Laodicean Trap #3: Indifference

The Laodicean strand of the church offers God without repentance and church without the Kingdom. Thus, the church is powerful and independent and preaches another gospel. Thus, the message is affirming rather than transforming. How can this be? If we are preaching the same gospel of Jesus and it got Him killed, why is the Laodicean message loved by sinners and believers alike? Jesus Himself stated that if He was hated, you too will be hated for His namesake. Why does the world feel so comfortable in the church of Laodicea? Well, because the church preaches a message of self-development vs. transformation to the image of Christ, and lest we forget, God has called each of us to be transformed by the renewing of our minds (Romans 12:1, 2). The altars of the cultural church do not create new converts that are child-like and entering the Kingdom of God according to John 3:33-35 and Matthew 18:1-5. Once people join, the Laodicean church refuses or cannot hear the voice of Christ the King so they preach what the people want to hear. As a result, current statistics suggest that the majority of Christians are biblically illiterate and don't actively seek to understand the scriptures.[18]

Thus, the predominant characteristic of the sociological church today, represented in Revelation 3:15-20, is neutrality to things of the spirit — neither cold nor hot but lukewarm to scripture, God's will, and Kingdom living. Its members are simply church-goers but not soldiers of the Lord. They do not read or study the Bible for spiritual growth and development; they are the embodiment of James 1:22-26 - hearers of the Word and not doers, deceived by themselves. Many church folk admire people that are literally God-haters, as defined by scripture as the carnally minded and friends of the world. Church folks purchase products that fight against the church. They could care less as long as it's the most economic choice. Neutrality is the message of the church. Ask a person who goes to a Laodicean church why they attend and they will tell you that it makes them feel good about themselves. Not to become better equipped to be a witness for Christ but encouraged and affirmed! Then you have others that acknowledge to the world that they do not know the Bible and are not concerned with doctrine.

People are attracted to the Laodicean church because its focus is self. Members enjoy being motivated to a higher level of living through either the accumulation of financial resources or the acquisition of knowledge. The latter, however, is a form of modern-day gnosticism, a teaching declared heretical in the 1st century. They are always learning but never coming to the knowledge of the truth, which is you must live your life for God and not self. "How can God help me live larger, get more, and be blessed?" messages predominate, and are designed to make you feel good about yourself. The doors of the church are closed!

I stood and preached "The Doors of the Church are Closed" at a church and the people went ballistic! Their spirits in agreement, they responded enthusiastically and positively. The pastor looked at them and as soon as I handed him the microphone, the first words that came out of his mouth (after I had just taught them that God gave us the keys to the Kingdom and they were wrongly opening the doors of the church) was "The doors of the church are open..." There are people trapped in the church and they are so trapped through tradition, through rituals, through social issues that Jesus is standing outside and saying "if any man hears my voice and opens the door, I come in to him..."

Today, we face what Augustine referred to in his book, *City Of God* as phenomena of the visible and the invisible church. The invisible church is God's true church and its members worship and serve God amidst those who are simply a part of the visible church. Augustine posits that you can be a part of the visible church but not a part of the invisible church, but if you are a part of the invisible church, you will be a part of the visible church. Simply put, Augustine wanted us to know that everybody in church is not saved, but everybody that's saved is in church. When this life is over, visible church members will reap the consequence of eternal separation from God and not the benefit of eternal life with God. You must evaluate the visible church you attend and whether or not you are a member of the invisible church.

Our eternal destination is not a secret; the Bible says examine the scriptures to see if you are in the faith. What is mind numbing is that in the sociological church, the Bible is either no longer being preached or misappropriated for the advancement of self-will and not the will of God. The average Christian has either no understanding or a skewed understanding of the Bible and the concept of God. To the church's chagrin, the laity has embraced the spirit of the historical church, which over the years taught people that the Bible is not important. Therefore, when you go to the average church, you'll hear a Scripture read, then everybody shuts his book and something else is talked about. Fables and stories are told, and in some cultures, you get three points and a poem. Then, in other cultures, you get three points and a whoop, but none of the points point you to the King.

When we consider the alarming statistics that point to the ignorance of Christians concerning biblical concepts and understanding, Christ no longer has the affection of the contemporary church. On the contrary, when you look at Christian TV, you don't hear about Christ and His Kingdom but how to establish your own kingdom on earth. The church simply speaks to the needs and the desires of its members, not its King. Church members even say, "I want to go someplace where I feel comfortable. I need to go some place that meets my needs."

Consequently, people do not know what it means to be out of the will of God nor the consequence — hell. The sociological church preaches that church membership and attendance is all you need to see Jesus in heaven. Now, there was a time when messages on hell would scare you into heaven, but since hell is no longer preached, people, in the midst of financial difficulties and relational challenges, say that they are catching hell right now. However, that's not the hell that Jesus talked about. Hell is eternal separation from God. The doors of the church are closed and either you're on the outside with the King of Kings and the Lord of Lords, or you're trapped in tradition on the inside. If you remain inside, ignorant to His will, your destiny will be amongst those that do not go with Jesus and find yourself saying, 'Lord, Lord, did I not prophecy in your name? Did I not work on an usher board? Was I not on the trustee board? Did I not sing in the choir? Wasn't I a musician? Wasn't I the head of the soprano section? Wasn't I this, that, and the other?' And He will say to you, "Depart from Me, you worker of iniquity, for I do not know you." (Matthew 7:21)

In Revelation 4:1,2, Jesus is still outside knocking. Then John is snatched up in the Rapture, another dispensation. The church age has ended and the invisible church is no longer on earth. Now, John is at an open door and when he walks through the open door, he sees the environment of a kingdom.

What is this kingdom? This is the Kingdom of God. So what am I saying? The majority of today's churches are going to be uninterrupted when the true church is raptured. That's one of the reasons people are not going to believe in the Rapture because there are going to be so many church folks still here. The Bible says that except a man is born again, he cannot enter into the Kingdom. I'm a firm believer in cause and effect, and there's a reason why the sociological church does not preach about the Kingdom [please visit my website and order my series entitled, "Unlocking the Mysteries of the Kingdom of God."]. It's a dangerous thing to think your eternal destination is secured because you sacrifice one day a week to come to church and listen to somebody preach at you.

Interestingly, the majority of people that attend the Laodicean strand of church come for a variety of reasons that are totally unrelated to the central mission and call of the church and the gospel of the Kingdom. Apparently, many church goers are trying to appease another kind of standard or normative behavior in their psyche because coming to church for reasons other than Christ's is nonsensical. When we go to church, we are supposed to come to hear a word from the King. So if the King's word doesn't mean anything, then why come in the first place? You might as well stay home, turn on the boob tube, get you a half a pint of beer, put your legs up and get drunk and wait for the fire.

The other strand of the church consists of those believers who are loyal to Christ as King and see themselves, not as a cultural people, but as the people of God and the body of Christ that exists solely to fulfill the King's will upon the earth. These people are the people whom I refer to as the remnant, i.e., those that have really experienced Christ as Lord and Savior. The Body of Christ is juxtaposed between polar opposites — the cultural, sociological church vs. the Kingdom church. The cultural church appeals to people that never repent and die to themselves to fulfill the life of Christ the King — they come to join the church. Now this is significant because people are joining the cultural church by the thousands, week after week, without coming to a real salvific appreciation of what happened at the cross. They never come to the altar acknowledging their sin nature and Christ's redemptive work on the cross for their sin. They never acknowledge the fact that He died a vicarious death for them. Thus, the sinless death of Christ or the sinless life of Christ does not matter to the average church person. The virgin birth does not matter to the average church person. The physical and bodily resurrection of our Lord does not matter to the average church person because the redemptive life of Christ that He gave on the cross of Calvary does not matter to the average church person.

After all, the person in the cultural church is just simply joining the church. The person in the cultural church never experiences conversion; they simply commit to the local church, which is governed by either the will of people or a desire to fit into society. In many places, this church has essentially been mutated into a "group counseling center" where all the messages are geared towards healing people of what they should have been delivered from at the cross! Messages address issues in people who have never died. God never designed or intended the entirety of our Christian life to be a lifelong exercise in healing and deliverance from our past. The average church service seems like one big group counseling session. The people have not truly died to themselves or their past. Instead, this type of multi-dysfunctional environment allows persons to constantly carry their past pain and even nurture their past pain, latent with bitterness and resentment.

Its leadership and focus is on the accumulation of members — much like health clubs or other social institutions — rather than the production of disciples who are appreciative of Christ for their salvation and serve Him as Lord. The opening of church doors has created people who are self-serving, self-centered, and self-obsessed. That is because the opening of the doors of the church allowed the wrong things in. Culture, class, currency issues, creations of the flesh, and other carnal compromises rushed through the doors. The church we have come to know is a church that has been divided by lines of race, class, and culture, all socio-economic terms. Rather than tearing down such barriers and everyone sharing one heart, one mind, and one dominate activity (Acts 2:42-47), the phenomenon of the church doors simply incorporates these divisions into its fiber, fabric, and cultural make up. Rather than become the Body of Christ that reflects Christ and His Kingdom, the church persists to be cultural representatives of sex biases, class preferences, race prejudices, and denomination superiority. The doors of the church are closed!

American Protestantism Defiled

The church of Laodicea has permeated all areas of the Christian church, even though many of the Laodicean traps named above characterize churches in the contemporary evangelical branch of Protestantism. However, the prejudices of the church followed the believers that colonized America and set up the mainline Protestant churches here. Unfortunately, the members of the denominational churches have not been told the truth concerning the perversion of their biblical position either. The effects of an open door church have skewed the message of God in their practices as well. While some of these churches would not consider themselves Laodicea, because they don't teach a wealth and increase message, they are blinded to the ungodly ways they accumulated their wealth. The mainline churches don't teach a wealth and increase message. However, they taught and still teach a message of cultural and spiritual superiority that suppressed and enslaved a people. This system allowed them to gain economic wealth and advantage, particularly in America. In America, the mainline churches supported a governmental system that enslaved, abused, and murdered innocent people to establish wealth, then proclaimed their wealth as the favor of God. The gospel of Jesus Christ was skewed for political acceptance and economic gain. The issue is those who are in the mainline churches were connected politically and given unfair advantages concerning property and wealth.

The wealth and increase ministers are those who were not from the highest class of whites in America, along with minority preachers who had been locked out of the mainstream of economic opportunity. Yet those who gained their wealth through the exploitation of Africans in the slave trade are guilty of the same spirit and represent the foundation for the Laodicean church. Racial superiority was practiced on the plantation as well as the church. Thus, the Laodiceans are characterized as wretched, miserable, poor, blind, and naked. The practice of slavery and the categorization of Africans as three-fifths of a man was wretched. The fact that blacks were relegated to pre-Adamite status in order to justify their mistreatment of human beings was wretched. The castration of men, the prevention of stable marriages and families, separation of parents from children, and the rape of both men and women for economic and social benefit of a people was wretched.

The gravest aspect of the wretchedness of the mainline churches was the fact that significant denominations ignored the issue and remained silent, while teaching a compassionate gospel. Laodicea is not simply made up of slick-dressing white and black preachers, but of the politically correct white clergy who act one way in public and dress up in white sheets in private. When you are supposed to be the institution that represents truth and justice and allow philosophies that espouse that one ethnic group is superior to another and qualify cultural traits as moral or of a higher value than others — this is wretched. Unfortunately, when people think about Laodicea, they only see those who are trying to work their way from the bottom of the barrel to a higher level of economic opportunity and privilege and fail to acknowledge the millions of dollars of endowments from real estate and industry that was given to empty main-line churches, but gained from the blood, sweat, and tears of enslaved Africans and the American slavery system. God sees what is done in the dark and He repays (Luke 12:1-3) in the light. You cannot manipulate geography, history, anthropology, biology, sociology, and psychology for the sole benefit of a race and not know that it is wretched, unless you are blind. Note: blindness is another characteristic of Laodicea.

Consequently, the colonists brought the images of a European Christ to portray God. The open door of America allowed Europeans to make themselves the image of God and they had a picture to prove it. Cultural superiority, devoid of facts, has misled the world into believing Jesus, a Jew, was a white man. Martin Luther declared that images create idols in the mind – idols for white people (white superiority) and idols for black people (black inferiority). The Laodicean mainline churches developed another gospel to support their philosophy. Very few churches were bold enough to tear down these idols, reject this new gospel, and proclaim Christ as Lord for all people (some Quakers and Puritans were abolitionists). Some denominations did split as a result of disagreements over the institution of slavery such as the Methodist Episcopal Church in 1844 and the Presbyterian Church in 1837 and 1857. As a backlash to 'white' Christianity, African-American religions were formed: the Nation of Islam and the Shrine of the Black Madonna, etc. We will never know how many souls failed to enter the Kingdom of God because they perceived Jesus Christ to be "white" and His churches unrepentant for its involvement in the American slavery system. Christ said in Mark 9:42:

> *But whoever causes one of these little ones who believe in Me to stumble, it would be better for him if a millstone were hung around his neck, and he were thrown into the sea. (Mark 9:42)*

You will not hear the truth of its history in the Laodicean mainline churches. The devil knows that the way to stop the average black preacher from preaching truth is to send a non-black person to his church. One non-black person in a congregation of blacks will change the direction of an entire message. If it doesn't, the congregants will get offended for the non-black. Why? Because blacks are programmed, from slavery, to protect and cow tow to white people. Nevertheless, the Laodicean church must acknowledge its wrong doing, either through commission or omission. If you have benefited from social injustice in the name of God, you are guilty of a serious crime against the Kingdom of God. If someone breaks in the bank and steals money and gives it to you, once you accept the money, you are now guilty of the crime, especially if you know how it was obtained. Either we are a part of the problem or a part of the solution; there is no middle ground.

This type of presentation of Christianity also created a social movement in the black community called the oasis syndrome — an escape from the cruel harsh and unjust affairs of the white culture. In America, the church segregated along the lines of race, creating white churches and black churches, purely social institutions. While the church under black leadership has advanced the cause of social justice, an emphasis on the Word of God and the Great Commission does not prevail. Many of them have become churches of style and not substance. For example, how can you be a 'missionary' Baptist church and no one has left the community? Style but no substance! Many of the Black churches have become fashion shows, musical entertainment, and places of pomp and circumstance. Due to the lack of spiritual focus and only social focus, some blacks came into the things of God and have ghettoized the Kingdom. They have violated God's governmental order and authority – locking pastors out the church, participating in fistfights, bringing firearms to church meetings, etc. African-Americans have turned the house of God into a mess of chicken dinners, annuals, debutante balls, and all kinds of social affairs that do not have a thing to do with God or His Kingdom. The doors of the church are closed!

I hope that if you are reading this book, you are reading with an objective mind, not one on the defense. Whether we desire to face it or not, we live in a nation that is race-driven. Those who name the name of Christ as Lord, however, are to relate to each other, not on the basis of race, but the spirit. This cannot simply be a phenomenon that takes place on one side of the bridge but among all people. Just imagine how much of a witness we would be if the world saw that believers in America had been delivered from the effects of racism and were coming together!

The problem is simple. So-called believers refuse to define themselves by the Kingdom. Let's take one of the greatest denominations of our country, Southern Baptist, who are called Southern Baptist because they broke from the Georgian Baptist Movement when they refused to give up their slaves. The reason there is a National Baptist Convention (black) is because of the segregated Baptist Church that did not allow people of color to join. The reason why we have the Assemblies of God religion is because whites refused to continue to be ordained by the Church of God in Christ, the first Pentecostal Church, under the leadership of Charles Mason, a black man. While there have been some apologies made, there has not been the retraction of a racist theology of separatism nor elitism.

Laodicea is a dangerous place to be, for it accentuates the bait of Satan to the highest degree. He uses the pride of life, the lust of the flesh, and the lust of the eyes (1 John 2:15-16). The American Church, from its inception, fell for the old garden trick. You know — the same one he used on Eve. What is it? You can be like God (superiority) and you will have the knowledge of good and evil (subjectivism and relativism). He told the early American church that you can serve both God and mammon — the Protestant work ethic and the spirit of capitalism. My brothers and sisters, come out of the church mentality and embrace your Kingdom assignment. We have all been lied to and Christ is standing at the door knocking. His favor is leaving the North American continent and taking up residence on other continents. We cannot continue to let the color of our skin keep us divided. Unfortunately, whenever people talk about integration in the Body, they are really saying "you can come back to the plantations." So-called believers refuse to define themselves by the Kingdom and insist on defining themselves by race and run to the socially-approved church, which is the residue of the state church.

Eurocentrism has governed Christendom in America as though Europeans are the official keepers of the faith and codified the European race as a reflection of God. We have a very ugly and turbulent past in the American church, but we must acknowledge and re-teach a sound doctrine of the Kingdom. God gave us an opportunity to repent under the leadership of Dr. King, the Apostle of love, non-violence, and unity through justice. But to the Kingdom's chagrin, Dr. King was not joined in his marches by Protestant preachers, black or white. Billy Graham and Oral Roberts did not march with him, instead a Roman Catholic priest and a Jewish rabbi marched. Where was the church that was founded upon one Lord, one faith, and one baptism (Ephesians 4:5)? Unless racism in the church of Laodicea is dealt with, believers in Jesus Christ will remain divided.

Satan has been so masterful; he has sewn this thing up where nobody can speak about the church's dirty laundry without being labeled. No prophet, no man of God can say these things without seeming like he's a racist. I know this kind of talk makes many of my African-American brothers and sisters quite uneasy. However, there may be as many Europeans ready for this truth as African-Americans. Yet, some African-Americans are so protective of the dominant race that when you hear something like this they start looking around and feeling bad for whites. Sadly, protecting white people has been instilled in some black people and this mentality is deeply engrained in the fabric of the black mind. However, I must speak because the white preacher is not going to preach about it because he's benefiting. The message of the Promise Keepers is we've got to reconcile. Well, when is the last time you heard their preachers telling their members, who are racist, that they need to get out of these churches and go and fellowship with other churches and Christians of different races who are all a part of God's Kingdom? We must understand that this church mentality is not an issue of skin; it is an issue of sin. Wake up and hear the voice of Jesus amidst all of your formalized hymnal singing and your polished and quiet worship services. Christ is knocking on the door of the church and attempting to usher those who will respond into the Kingdom.

We are living in what I consider to be the most spiritually dangerous time in Christianity because the contemporary Christian church is at a crossroads. We're living in what can be called the age of compromise and deception. Unless extreme measures are taken to seek the Kingdom of God, you are in more danger in the church then you could ever be outside of it. Those that are a part of the church of Laodicea are called wretched, miserable, poor, blind, and naked by Christ. This church is sternly instructed to be transformed by the power of Christ, the cross, and His righteousness. In Revelation, the beloved disciple John reveals that by the end of the church age, Christ will be standing at the door of the church, knocking and seeking entrance into the hearts of individuals that still have the capacity to hear and recognize His voice, but the outcome is not clearly mentioned. As you listen to the text, you hear what He is saying to those who hear Him: "I will come in..." Jesus emphasizes 'hearing' His knock because now hearing is scarce. Hearing is scarce because hearing the voice of God is hearing the Word of God and the Word of God is not being preached in the contemporary church, referred to, but not proclaimed and explained.

I know that it makes a lot of people feel extremely nervous and uncomfortable when they hear me make the emphatic proclamation about the church. I can feel you even as I write! After all, the church has historically meant a lot to all of us. Nostalgia and the many positive neurological associations that come to mind regarding the church secures a special place in our hearts for her. While this has been a very sensitive and critical issue in our contemporary society, the fact still remains that whether or not I pronounce those doors closed or not, Christ in Revelation 3:20 is still standing at the door knocking! Whether we like it or not, the undeniable implication of this scripture is that people are having church and Jesus is not in the room!

Change and transition is very difficult. We all enjoy and are comfortable at some level with our sacred cows of the past. For good or ill, our sacred cows of the past have become our identity and our history; they are inextricably tied to who we have become. When I stand and proclaim that the doors of the church are closed I do so with careful prophetic analysis and theological investigation. I am not saying the doors of the church are closed due to my frustration with church nor to my lack of appreciation for what the church has done historically. I have a great appreciation for the church, as erroneous and as off as it may be spiritually. It is the bridge that has brought many of us to an understanding and an acceptance of the concept of God. It is the bridge that has brought some of us to the understanding of some of the general spiritual practices that we now engage in, such as prayer, devotion, fasting, and tithing.

The church that we have known in times past is now undergoing a final reformation. However, reformation is not the total abandonment of the church. Rather, it is the church undergoing a "behavior modification." Most importantly, it is the church redefining itself according to scripture verses culture. When the great reformer Martin Luther nailed his 95 theses to the door of the Castle Church in Wittenberg, Germany, it read, "Disputation of Dr. Martin Luther on the Power and the Efficacy of Indulgences by Dr. Martin Luther 1517."[15] He starts the 95 theses by saying,

"Out of love for the truth and the desire to bring it to light the following propositions will be discussed at Wittenberg, under the presidency of the Reverend Father Martin Luther, pastor of arts and sacred theology and lecturer in ordinary on the same at that place. Wherefore he requests those who are unable to be present and debate orally with us may do so by letter."[16]

He then wrote his 95 theses challenging Roman Catholicism. He was attempting to reform the church, not in condemnation, but because he saw the traditions of Rome had taken preeminence over Scripture. His reformation gave birth to and resulted in a new form of religious expression termed Protestantism.` Due to his movement, the Roman Catholic Church felt deeply threatened theologically. It refused to debate its traditions and practices, choosing instead to banish Martin Luther, who fled into exile because his life was threatened. It was only through the help of powerful friends like Frederick III, Elector of Saxony, also known as "Frederick the Wise", and Philipp Melanchthon, a German professor and theologian, that he escaped the clutches of the Roman Catholic Church. The courageous Luther did not reemerge again until the Peasant War of 1524. Note that Luther was moved by the Holy Spirit to challenge the entire Roman Catholic Church papal theology with the truth of scripture. Later, the Great Awakening produced the message of regeneration and its message focused on personal conversion, i.e., "you must be born again."

Beloved, today we are in the midst of another reformation. God is moving His church from where it is to where it needs to be. The church has been under observation by men of God throughout church history. Saint Augustine, Luther, Calvin, Wesley, Niebuhr and others have analyzed the church and found it lacking and have attempted to reform it. The integrity of the church has been entrenched since its subjection to the influence of the Roman Empire. Prior to its marriage to Rome, the New Testament church was a living organism that focused upon spreading the message of Christ and the Kingdom of God. Yet history teaches us through the experience of reformers like Martin Luther that the reformer's teachings are initially rejected, then followed by their ex-communication. They are roundly scoffed as heretics. Reformers are tough, passionate, and deeply devoted individuals. They are necessary and effective over time. The church is now in need of reform for the doors that Constantine the Great opened and western culture kept open, historically, are now closed. The culture-dominated church of today is not the church that Jesus built nor is it the one that He is at work in.

We are in transition, but transition is good! Christian Schwarz, a German Theologian, states in his book entitled, *Paradigm Shift in the Church*, that every reformation movement is confronted with an opposing force known as orthodoxy. This was the case in the days of the 16th century reformation in the Roman Catholic Church and in days of the Pietistic revival in Europe, and is also the case in today's contemporary churches. Schwarz saw this as the dispensation of a third reformation, the first reformation being led by Martin Luther, the second being the Pietistic led by George Whitfield, and Jonathan Edwards. I would add another reformation, the fourth reformation, led by William J. Seymour.

The question may be, "Has there ever been any good that has come out of the church?" And the answer to that is "Of course." The church always has and still is producing people that love God. However, the majority of churches are not producing disciples for Christ. They are creating financial support for the service of debt and the purpose of profit and increase. There are people getting saved in the church. Even in the Roman Catholic Church, people are born again/saved. However, their salvation is due neither to the vision or the context of the corporate church. People get saved because of the passion and aggression of select individuals who desire to know more about God. However, the church must change to conform itself to the originally intended Kingdom purposes of a Sovereign God – "Go therefore and make disciples of all the nations, baptizing them in the name of the Father and of the Son and of the Holy Spirit, teaching them to observe all things that I have commanded you; and lo, I am with you always, even to the end of the age." (Matthew 28:19, 20 – The Great Commission)

Outside the Church with Jesus

In the Laodicean era, God has raised up and is raising up Kingdom-minded churches that are replacing many of the failing churches, especially in North America. There are Kingdom-minded people being raised up by God that will be Great Commission-conscious. They will strive to go through every open door that God unlocks with the Key of David. This church is a church that is not consumed with Mercedes Benz' and mansions but is laying treasure in heaven by embracing the valuable work of the Kingdom. This church can be found executing Acts 1:8, ministering from home to the utter parts of the world. This church will be found preaching the Kingdom of God, which will also be the message of the 144,000 Jewish missionaries of Revelation 7:4, according to Matthew 24:14. In the church realm, the Roman Catholic Church is believed to be the whore of Babylon according to Revelation because of the serious compromises made in the name of imperialism and capitalism. The church that Jesus established was not established according to socio-economic parameters. According to the Scripture, the church that Jesus built in Matthew 16 was built so that the gates of Hades shall not prevail against it. As stated earlier, the Greek word for church is *ekklesia*. The word origin of this term is a combination of *ek* (out of, from, by, away from) and *kaleo* (kaleh'-o), which means to call, to call aloud, utter in a loud voice, to invite, to summons. The *ekklesia* is an assembly for worshippers called out of and away from the rest of the world. Such an assembly is thereby set apart and set aside for the King's purposes. Such an assembly desires to carry out His vision, which means that the church was created to carry out the vision of its owner. Whenever the church loses the vision of its owner, it ceases to be the church.

The church was not only created to carry His vision, but Jesus said "upon this rock I will *build*..." The Greek term for build is *oikodomeo*, and the root of that word is *oikos*. *Oikos* is the Greek term for house, an inhabited house. So, *oike-domeo* or "build" means inhabitation. Therefore, not only was the church, the *ekklesia,* designed to promote His vision, but it was also birthed to perpetuate His culture. The role of the church is to spread the culture of the Kingdom. Not only was the church designed to carry His vision and His culture, the church was designed to carry His keys, for He said that I give you the keys to the Kingdom.

Not only was the church designed to carry His vision, His culture and His keys, the church was also designed to exercise His authority, for He says that whatever you bind on earth will be bound in heaven and whatever you loose on earth will be loosed in heaven. Instead, the church has become weak, impotent, and anemic — all as a result of losing its vision. We suffer from diplopia, or double vision. We no longer know what the truth is because we've been blinded by culture, class, currency, and a whole host of issues that are the creation of flesh and compromise. The *ekklesia* was not just a distinct group of people functioning as a peculiar institution, but a living organism that carried His vision, His culture, His keys, and His authority. The *ekklesia* was comprised of the kind of people that yielded themselves to the voice of the Holy Spirit as God the Father was adding to the church daily (Acts 2:47).

Unfortunately, due to the social agenda of the church, the DNA of Christ was rejected and the social agenda of racism aborted the spread of the Kingdom culture. The church and the society lay in a state of total chaos and confusion. Since the theology of the contemporary church is so laced with cultural biases, even the most skilled North American theologian has a difficult time rightly dividing the word of truth. Imagine what messages are coming across the pulpit of theologians ignorant of the Kingdom of God! I propose that it is next to impossible for the church in North America to spread the culture of the Kingdom.

Make no mistake, the Christian church in America is strictly a black and a white mutation. You may ask, "Do you think a bridge will ever extend from the white culture into churches under black leadership like the bridge that extends from the black culture to churches under white leadership? What about Latinos or Asians?" I surely hope so because that is the Kingdom! The Kingdom of God is not the sociological church that reflects race, sex, and class. It is a united Kingdom where the Spirit reigns, not the flesh. These differences have prevented us from hearing Christ through whomever He wants to use. The average non-black cannot hear Christ through a black man because of the stereotypes and negative perceptions that have been created. The average black person is trained to hear the voice of a white leader before they hear a black leader. Thus, people are no longer hearing the voice of the King — He has been locked out and His culture is not the preferred culture. Thus, the church of Laodicea has said to Christ, "Keep a-knocking but you can't come in!" God is looking for disciples and worshippers, not Christians! God is seeking worshipers that can enter the Kingdom.

The doors of the church are closed but the gates of the Kingdom are available. The gates of the Kingdom of heaven are available for you, but you have to be born into the Kingdom. When you are born again, the first thing you ought to see is not the church. Jesus told Nicodemus except a man be born again, he cannot see the Kingdom. He said "Marvel not that I say unto you except a man be born again he cannot enter the Kingdom." (John 3:3) You cannot enter the Kingdom until you first see the Kingdom. If you've never seen the Kingdom, you cannot enter the Kingdom. It is imperative that everyone breaks out of the church. Heed my warning: it will be hard to leave the church mentality because now the doors of the church are closed, and the centuries and the guards, those who patrol the door, don't want to let you out. Cultural, racial, classist and denominational loyalty demands will be hurled at you. Jesus' prayer was "Father, make them one" – unfortunately, that is not the state we are in. We must stop recruiting people to come to church based upon denominational affiliations and cultural affiliations. Denominations and cultural allegiances create divisions in the church that are not supported in the Word of God. No one or thing should be able to trump the will of Jesus, the King, in your life - He must reign in the hearts and minds of men.

The doors of the church are closed. You need to tell everyone you can while they have a chance, GET OUT! You'd better come into the Kingdom, because Jesus never preached you into the church. He preached you into the Kingdom. As long as we are in the church, we will never ever be unified and neither will we ever execute the will of our Lord. Thus, in order to have a unified Kingdom, we must officially serve notice that the doors of the church are closed. Martin Luther attempted to close them. John Calvin attempted to close them. Ulrich Zwingli attempted to close them. John Wesley and Charles Wesley attempted to close them. Other Great Awakening preachers attempted to close them. William J. Seymour attempted to close them, but the only reason they could not close the doors of the church was because it was not the dispensation of the Kingdom. The reason we announce that the doors are closed in the 21st century is because we now have an alternative. We now can usher the people into the Kingdom, but they must exit the church and get out! The church is still an important institution upon the earth; however, it is imperative that we begin to redefine our idea of church because of what it has grown into. We must then relearn and understand the church of Jesus Christ through the prism or the lens of the Kingdom of God. Churches must allow God to reform their theology from a traditional sociologically-informed theology to a Kingdom of God theology.

THE KEYS OF THE KINGDOM ARE AVAILABLE

We are now at the threshold of Kingdom reform. We are transitioning from a church mentality to a Kingdom mentality. God is bringing us to a place of spiritual decision where we must choose whether He is servant or King. We must decide whether we exist for His purpose or does He exist to meet our needs. I must warn you, as King, He will totally govern your life, but what is the alternative? If we see Him as our servant, sent to meet our every need, He will allow us to live a life without Him. However, without Christ as King, we will receive the penalty that a life not focused on God deserves, and that is death. So, just in case anyone is confused, He is our One True King and He left us with a mandate! Matthew clearly states that the church was given the responsibility to open the gates of the Kingdom to all mankind.

We have discussed some of the things that have come through the doors of the church that have had both positive and negative effects in the Body of Christ. The church has experienced extreme flux for identity throughout the years due to its desire to be accepted by the world. As a result, the church has failed at achieving its Kingdom mandate. Now, according to the prophetic time lines of God and the events in time and history, the doors of the church are closed. That statement alone suggests that we must explore several areas in detail. As I mentioned previously, Jesus is the door and no man comes to the Father except by Him. In John 10:7 and John 10:9, Jesus states that He is the door of the sheep and that anyone who enters by the door will be saved. We now know that the Lord Jesus Christ is man's Redeemer, his Savior, and his propitiation. Desiring to reconcile the world back to Himself because of His love, God gave His only begotten Son. And those that die to themselves and live for Christ through faith, believers born again into the Kingdom of God, will gain eternal life with Him.

These believers make up the *ekklesia* or the church. They live for two primary reasons: evangelism and discipleship-making – they share the good news of Christ's redemption to the world and then they help to conform believers of Christ into disciples of Christ. Jesus gave the church several tools to help them do their work: 1) the power to bind and loose, and 2) the keys to the Kingdom. It is important for us to see the congruency between the church possessing the keys to the Kingdom and Jesus as the door.

So let's examine a number of scriptures as we discuss the keys to the Kingdom. In Matthew 16:18 the Word reads:

> *"And I also say to you that you are Peter, and on this rock I will build My church, and the gates of Hades shall not prevail against it." 16:19 reads: "... and I will give you the keys of the kingdom of heaven, and whatever you bind on earth shall be bound in heaven, and whatever you loose on earth shall be loosed in heaven."*
>
> *Now to the book of Revelation, where chapter 3:7 records: "And to the angel of the church in Philadelphia write, 'These things says He who is*

*holy, He who is true, "He who has the key of David,
He who opens and no one shuts, and shuts and no
one opens"*

*Lastly, let's look remember our seminal passage
in Revelations 3:20, "Behold, I stand at the door and
knock. If anyone hears My voice and opens the door,
I will come in to him and dine with him, and he with
Me."*

The church possessing the keys to the Kingdom denotes
that the church has been given the responsibility of introducing people to Christ the King and His Kingdom. When
someone comes to Jesus, they come to Him and die. In the
words of that noted German theologian Dietrich Bonheoffer
from his book, *The Cost of Discipleship*, "When Christ bids
a man to come, He bids him to come and die." [20] This man
loved God and His people so much that he willingly chose
to die in a Nazi concentration camp during the Holocaust
because of his confession of faith. While he was a professor
at Union Theological Seminary, he chose to travel back to
Germany just to go in the fire with those that were sacrificing
their lives.

The Gospel we receive today is "Come unto Me and
live." Yet before you can have an abundant life, you must
have an abundant death. The Word of God says that you were
crucified with Christ. So when you perceive the degrading
death that Christ died on the cross and you see Him dying
the death that you deserved to die, you must identify with
that death and put yourself on the cross with Him. You must
do that because it was your sin that nailed Him there, but
it was His love that kept Him there. You die by confessing
your sin nature, your sin guilt, and your sin sentence; you
died and then were born again. You are born again as an
alien in a foreign land because you were born again in the
Kingdom of God, a stranger from another world. At the

point of your salvation, you see the Kingdom. When you took your first step, you stepped into the Kingdom. Thus, you are a Kingdom citizen.

Ephesians 2:6 said that when you got saved as a new creation, you were made to sit with Christ Jesus in heavenly places. Your citizenship is in the Kingdom of God. But you are a dual citizen, just like Paul was a Roman citizen and a citizen of the Kingdom. In the natural, you may be an American, Nigerian, or Indian citizen, but in the spirit, you are a citizen of the Kingdom of God and your spiritual life and citizenship takes preeminence over your natural life and citizenship.

The church of Laodicea is no longer open to the idea of existing for the purpose of introducing people to Christ the King and His Kingdom. Christ is the door to God, as we mentioned, so just imagine what it looks like to see Christ knocking on the door of the church when He is the doorway to God. The church was designed and appointed to be the official delegate of the Kingdom of God and Christ is the door that allows people entry but He Himself has been locked out of the church. I cannot stress more strongly how significant the doors of the church being closed are. There are millions of people inside those doors that don't realize that Christ is the door to the Kingdom and when you leave Him outside, it is impossible to gain access to the Kingdom. Nonetheless Christ has been voted out of the church due to social and secular interests.

Literally, the church was tasked with the ability to connect people to the Kingdom of God through the proclamation of Christ and His saving grace. The next responsibility is to disciple them to be followers of Christ and not Christians. "Christian" is somewhat of a misnomer. It is not an appropriate name for a follower of Christ. [I don't necessarily see it as a negative word, but I just see it as a disempowering word.] The term was first used in Acts 11 in Antioch.

"And when he had found him, he brought him to Antioch. So it was that for a whole year they assembled with the church and taught a great many people. And the disciples were first called Christians in Antioch." (Acts 11:26)

Taking a closer examination demonstrates that the term "Christian" is a word that believers in the early church, rarely, if ever, referred to themselves as. (The lone exception is Peter's reference in 1 Peter 4:16: "Yet if anyone suffers as a Christian, let him not be ashamed, but let him glorify God in this matter.") They were called Christians by the people in Antioch, but in almost all other instances, they called themselves disciples. This is much more than hyper-technical nitpicking. A different psychological shift takes place when you call yourself a Christian vs. calling yourself a disciple. When you're a Christian, you can just "be", but when you're a "disciple", you have to *do*. I believe that the devil has used the word "Christian" to deceive millions throughout history about our true identity. The title Christian is the reason people can feel comfortable as "Christians" and never evangelize or make one disciple. Now it is time to use the word disciple. Christ was always very precise in His word usage and in Matthew 28:19, He did not say "Go ye therefore and make Christians"; He said "Go ye therefore and make *disciples*." The root word for disciple in the Greek is *manthano* which means "to learn, be appraised, to increase one's knowledge, to be increased in knowledge to hear, be informed, to learn by use and practice, to be in the habit of, accustomed to." Christ was intentional in conveying the proactive lifestyle He desired of such a person and the serious nature of the relationship that existed between Him and those who profess Him.

In contrast, the term "Christian" has become a socially politicized word that has caused us to backslide as disciples. The word Christian only appears in texts that speak of believers from an outsider's point of view. Christian was never a revelation of God but a revelation of outsiders. For example, in Acts 26:28, King Agrippa responded to Paul's eloquent discourse with, "You almost persuade me to become a Christian." (descriptive term offered by the King, not by Paul). So, this revelation by those outside the faith is what we have ended up calling ourselves and is what we've been calling ourselves throughout history since the doors of the church were opened by Constantine the Great in 312 AD. However, the overwhelming balance of scripture does not suggest that we are 'Christians'.

Not grasping our true identity makes it easy for us to refer to America as a Christian nation without even blinking an eye. We are what other people say about us, but we are not what Christ has called us to be, *disciples*. When will we become a nation of disciples? You hear the term church in the gospel three times and the word 'Christian' three times. As a result, we have something we term 'the Christian church' but we forget about Kingdom disciples. Over the centuries, we have lost sight of the fact that this name is a social term — Christian Church— that was given great power and efficacy in the Roman Empire under Constantine the Great. To be a Roman citizen was to be a Christian and to be a Christian was to be a Roman citizen. They were synonymous. So, therefore, you didn't have to be converted. All you had to be was a Christian. In America, the same process of thought permeates our society and I am strongly convinced that this is one of the reasons many 'so-called' Christians know absolutely nothing about conversion or their purpose for existence.

Christ called us to be converted and become disciples; however, it just seems so weird for someone to call themselves a disciple when they are not making a disciple. How can you be a disciple that's not making a disciple? How can you disciple without a mentee? We see the idiocy of this mental masturbation when we look at it in other contexts. What if your surgeon knew nothing about surgery but was a tree farmer instead? When was the last time you bought a car from a car dealer who did not deal in cars? Or bought meat from a butcher who had no meat? Are we in the habit of buying our utilities from a utility company that leaves us in the dark and without power? This term Christian has us twisted all around, playing a dangerous game of make believe that has eternal consequences for us and those who rely on us. Maybe if we get rid of the word Christian, we would really be about our Father's business. Maybe we will stop smoking the church's dope, claiming we are something we are not. In Acts, Christian is what they were called. Disciples are who they were. I realize the likelihood of replacing the name Christian with disciple is highly unlikely; however, it is the right thing to do for believers that have picked up their keys to the Kingdom.

The Lord wants you to think and rely on Scriptures for yourself now. It's time to pull away from all the time honored traditions that were birthed by a mutated, perverted church. As a theologian, pastor, and gospel preacher for over 20 years, I readily admit that I have been taught concepts that I've never questioned before. I just went along with the flow, like many of you. But thank God for His Word. Even though the disciples were called Christians in Antioch, in Acts11: 29, they are called disciples; and in Acts 14:20-22, 28; 15:10; 15:52; 18:23,27; 19:9; 20:1,7; and 21:4,16, they refer to themselves as disciples. Christ said make disciples and the early church started calling each other disciples, but what happened with us? The doors of the church opened under Constantine and begin to turn the idea and definition of a "Christian" into a passive catch-all phrase that anyone could slip on as a matter of status and convenience. Being a Christian became the "in-crowd" thing to do and the idea of conversion, discipleship, and what Jesus intended was lost in the translation.

While it is true that the doors of the church are closed, this is not a surprise to God; He knew it would happen before it did and wrote about it. The church is simply operating according to its dispensational destiny. However, there exists a remnant of those who are a part of God's true church that are distinct from the Laodicean or popular church that have their roots in the church of Philadelphia. There are still believers that identify with the Kingdom mission of the church. The church of Philadelphia became the foundation for the modern Kingdom-minded church that maintained their sensitivity to soul winning. This remnant will be very interested in the clarion call of the Kingdom.

While the Kingdom message is being re-introduced to the contemporary church, many sincere churches are still ignorant of the teaching of the Kingdom. The only way that the church can function properly as the custodian of the Kingdom of God is to learn about the Kingdom of God. These churches that heed the call that are a part of God's true church are not opening the doors of the church — they are opening the gates of the Kingdom. The Kingdom-minded church focuses upon making disciples and executing global missions. The Kingdom-minded church understands as disciples of Jesus Christ that we have been charged with preaching the gospel of the Kingdom of God and ushering in the second coming of Christ. Until that happens, the keys are made available to us for use. If the church does not use the keys to allow people entrance into the Kingdom, the church has lost its reason for being. The Kingdom-minded church accepts and embraces her call as an official representative of the Kingdom, an embassy of the Kingdom of God. The church exists at the pleasure of the Kingdom in order to represent the government of the Kingdom.

An Embassy of Heaven

As discussed earlier, the Bible teaches us that the role of the Christian Church is acting as an outpost of the Kingdom of God on earth. In essence, the church operates similar to a modern day embassy. The assignment of the church as an embassy is the ministry of reconciliation. Thus, Paul refers to himself as an ambassador and those who serve in the embassy as ministers of foreign affairs (2 Corinthians 5:18-20). The role of the ambassador is to equip the saints for the work of this ministry, according to Ephesians 4:12. Hence, Paul saw the church as the embassy and whenever the church stops being the embassy, it stops being the church. The embassy's sole purpose is to reflect the philosophies of its sending and supporting country on foreign soil. The embassy is responsible for handling all of the governmental business of its sending government on foreign soil. The embassy is the King's domain on foreign soil. That is why the Scripture constantly speaks in terms of us not being from this place. The Bible calls us pilgrims, sojourners, and foreigners. It says that we have a house that is not made by the hands of man, but made by God. Jesus said, "I go away to prepare a place for you." Accordingly, our place is not here; we are aliens, we do not belong to this world (1 Peter 2:10-11). Therefore, when we look at the Kingdom of God as our homeland and the church as the embassy, the embassy's role is to reconnect a fallen humanity to the King. People don't know God because they have fallen out of relationship with Him, but we've got the keys to the Kingdom. People can get back into relationship with God *through you!*

We see throughout the book of Acts, the concept of the church as intended by God. The church in the Pauline epistles is clearly pictured as a church that is totally committed and submitted to the call, cause, and covenant of Christ. In Corinthians, Paul states that the church consists of those called to be saints, set aside for the sacred, not the secular.

> *"Paul, called to be an apostle of Jesus Christ through the will of God, and Sosthenes our brother, to the church of God which is at Corinth, to those who are sanctified in Christ Jesus, called to be saints, with all who in every place call on the name of Jesus Christ our Lord, both theirs and ours:" (1 Corinthians 1:1,2)*

The root word of saints is *hagios*, which means "holy, set aside." We are called to be saints, called to be set aside for sacred duty and not secular duty. In 1 Corinthians 6:1-4, Paul states we are called to judge by Kingdom standards. We are to settle disputes among ourselves and not submit to inferior secular courts. The secular cannot and should not judge the sacred. Paul, in 1 Corinthians 11:18, describes within the concept of the Lord's Supper, the spiritual focus we are to have when we assemble so that the gathering does not devolve into a social gathering. Paul states that we can eat and socialize at home. He saw that the Corinthian saints were getting misfocused. You see, these saints were coming to church for the Lord's supper and the next thing you know they are all arguing over who gets the biggest piece of chicken and then falling out over food. So Paul told them to keep the social stuff at home.

The following are some expectations of an embassy of the Kingdom of God. Paul viewed the church as being called to establish the Kingdom or apostolic order. He writes in 1 Corinthians 12:28 that God set in the church Five-fold Ministry gifts for this purpose. He saw the church as a place of apostolic succession and order. He taught that the church is called to prophetic edification and that the prophetic word and the prophetic voice of the Lord is supposed to go forth in the embassy. (1 Corinthians 14:4,5 and 12) He saw the embassy or the church called to a clear and understandable spiritual communication. (1 Corinthians 14:19, 23 and 28)

[This is his discussion about tongues vs. clear communication.] The embassy is supposed to be a place where people can come and understand our message. Most that come to our churches today have no idea what the essence of Christianity is about. In Ephesians 1:22, Paul speaks of the church as Christ's Body with Christ as the head. The church is meant to be the place where the manifold wisdom of God is made known. (Ephesians 3:8-10) It is the place where Christ is given glory. (Ephesians 3: 21) Christ purchased and purged the church with His blood and will present the church without spot or wrinkle. In analyzing the relationship of Christ and His church to husbands and wives, Paul states in Ephesians 5:26, 27 that Christ nourishes and cherishes the church. (Ephesians 5:29) Paul says that it is the role of the church to economically support the work of the Kingdom. (Philippians 4:15)

The church is also a place where a certain standard of conduct is expected and a place of proven leadership. Paul specifically wrote "so that you may know how you ought to conduct yourself in the House of God." (1 Timothy 3:15) A prospective bishop or deacon must first rule his own house orderly and well before being a leader in Christ's Church. (1 Timothy 3:4-12) The church is the possession of the living God. Hebrews 10:23, 25 describes the church as a place of assembly for edification, admonishment, and exhortation. James wrote that the church was a place of praise, a place of prayer, and a place where the sick can call for the elders of the church to pray for them. (James 5:13-16)

The main work of the church is reconciliation and discipleship-making. When people give their life to Christ they become Kingdom citizens with a Kingdom mandate to spread the message of their sponsoring Kingdom (Colossians 1:13-14; Ephesians 2:19-22). As long as those who are sent to represent the Kingdom effectively perform their job, their needs will be provided for by the Kingdom government. This is how embassies operate. The needs of its citizens are taken care of if they are executing their assignment. This is why Christ states that if the believer prioritizes the Kingdom, all of his needs will be met (Matthew 6:33). Everyone that belongs to Christ's church is called to live as a Kingdom citizen and serve through the church. Thus, I live in the Kingdom and I work in the church.

The church operates as an embassy and has the express responsibility of taking care of the business of God. George Ladd in his book, *The Kingdom of God*, states that the church is the fellowship of disciples of Jesus who have received the life of the Kingdom and are dedicated to the task of preaching the gospel of the Kingdom in the world. Ladd continues to opine that the church is therefore not the Kingdom of God. God's Kingdom creates the church and works through the church. Men cannot build the Kingdom of God, but they can preach it and proclaim it. Upon hearing the good news of the Kingdom, a person can receive it or reject it. Hence, the Kingdom of God is the divine redemptive rule manifested in Christ; it is the realm and sphere in which the blessings of the divine rule may be experienced. The church is responsible for inviting people into that rule. Believers must get people in the rule of God. Therefore, the church is responsible for handling the keys to the Kingdom, not the doors of the church. The church is to lead people in salvation not membership. This is not a health club. This is not a fraternity. This is not the Lion's Club. This is not some distinguished gentlemen or distinguished ladies group. This is the embassy, a place where God is ruling and reigning in the reflection of His Kingdom.

The scripture proclaims that we have keys to the Kingdom, which suggests the church is the custodian of the Kingdom. We know that if we were to walk in a building complex and we saw someone with a large ring of keys, chances are they are the custodian. The custodian has been mandated to oversee his charge with authority and privileges others do not have. That's the reason people don't like keys because keys mean responsibility. So, when Jesus gave you the keys of the Kingdom, He gave you responsibility. If you are a part of the Church of the Lord Jesus Christ, Augustine's invisible church, you are supposed to have keys to the Kingdom. But if you don't have keys to the Kingdom, more than likely you are in the Laodicean church — not an embassy of God.

We've been designated to have keys. So where is your key? Your key suggests that you have authority; you have some type of right to enter or allow others' entrance. It also suggests that you have an assignment. You have a responsibility to let people in places they cannot get into on their own. The world is depending on the church to get them to heaven and instead the church is sending folks to hell because they're bringing them into their church membership and not Kingdom citizenship. The church is not ushering sinners into the Kingdom and it's going to be a sad day in eternity when so many people go to hell by way of the church. Your life is to be defined and determined by the King and His Kingdom, not the world and its worries. The world is depending on you and me. People don't meet Jesus the King in church. He is never introduced as the door – He's on the outside of the church knocking.

Looks can be deceiving, though! With the rise of the mega-church, it looks like things are going well in the church world. Unfortunately, statistics indicate this is not the case. The truth is that the church is totally ineffective as a witness for the Kingdom of God. Today, being a part of the church does not mean that one is saved nor does it mean that one has had any type of experience with Christ. Rather than ensuring that people are reconciled to Christ, the church has been racking up members for ego rather than souls for the Kingdom. The church is simply not bringing people to Christ in America.

Instead of the church engaging in the work of reconciliation and discipleship-making, the Church has given itself over to the god of mammon. Yet, despite the waywardness of the church, God has a remnant that has its roots in missionary theology; they understand the call of the Great Commission. God has obscure churches that will emerge and become very effective in their witness; I will discuss this position later.

Kingdom Ethnicity

People must be born into the Kingdom, which is a totally new race of people with a new identity and culture that totally differs from the world. It is not people joining up with people they think are better than they are or people that can glean a progressive spirit from or a people that they go to because they're sick of their own people. Nor is it a place that people go because they have been taught that others are inferior and to associate with them would be 'beneath them'. The Bible says that we are a holy nation, or *haggias ethnos*. Entering the Kingdom of God immediately changes our ethnicity to HOLY! Sadly, Christians choose to go through the doors of the church rather than walk through the gates of the Kingdom. The doors of the church offer sociological comforts that encompass our favorite 'isms (race, class, sex, and denomination). Yet in the Kingdom, His culture must prevail.

An excellent example of the importance of placing Kingdom culture above ethnicity is found in a 1st century occurrence. The Jerusalem church was the main church, which sent out ordained leadership for missions and ministry. The main church dispatched apostles and prophets in order to transform societies by sharing the Kingdom of God message. However, the Jerusalem council was tasked with mediating the Gentile inclusion dispute. They were responsible for trying to figure out how to integrate the Gentiles into the faith. Thus, the council simplified their responsibility by admonishing the Gentiles to simply stay away from food offered to idols or things offered to idols, from blood, from things strangled, and to stay clear of sexual immorality. However, these admonishments were tied to the kosher dietary laws of Israel and the fear that the Gentiles would offend Jewish Christians because of their eating habits. There was also a fear that the Gentiles would be persuaded by their former cultural experiences of the idol feast, celebrated by fornication. The Jerusalem Council worried that the Gentiles would further offend the Jewish Christian by being a part of the pagan feast, which involved selling and eating some of the animals that were sacrificed to gods at the market place.

Paul, however, corrected the Jerusalem Council when he said that the meat does not really matter. He told them to eat all of the meat they desired, but if meat offends your brother, don't eat it in front of him. In essence, what Paul was saying was that the Jerusalem Council had to mature in order to deal with this whole issue of integrating Gentiles into the faith. The Council was simply trying to appease the social demands of the Jewish religion, but in the process, they inappropriately attached cultural dictates to spiritual matters and raised such cultural preferences to a spiritual place of prominence. Through this experience and Paul's response, we learn an early lesson on the preeminence the Kingdom culture must have over any other group's natural culture. The doors of the church are closed, but the keys to the Kingdom are available.

We failed to reform the church in the past and now the doors of the church are officially closed and those who are stuck in its mentality will face a terrible future. I urge everyone to come out of the church of Laodicea, enter the Kingdom, and pick up your keys. "Dr. Carson, what will it take to create unity in the church world?" Heart-felt confession and Kingdom conversion. Our Kingdom bonds should reach deeper and broader than race, class, culture, and denomination. Until we all come to the knowledge of the truth and grow up and understand that He made from one blood many people, the enemy will continue to get an advantage over us (Acts 17:26). Additionally, if the church wants to become a powerful witness for Christ, leadership must seriously involve itself in the exegetical process and embrace a sound hermeneutical position concerning the interpretation of scripture. In essence, we must examine the original context and message of scripture and then examine its meaning for us today.

We must be aware of who has the keys to the Kingdom and what the keys are for. The Laodicean church, which consists of many of your independent charismatic churches, possess as their foundation, a quest for wealth. They don't have the keys nor do they desire to have the keys; they say they don't need them, for they have need of nothing. The church that emanated from the church of Philadelphia or the missionary movement picked up the keys to the Kingdom after they had been dropped in the 4th century and kicked to the 18th century and forgotten until the 21st century. If you have been a part of that church, you must ask yourself – "did I just join the church or am I born again?" If you do not know for sure (you may have been 'raised' in the church, baptized as a child, etc.) that you have been born again, you must repent and believe in the King as your Lord and Savior. He has been given a name that's above all other names, and at the name of Jesus, every knee shall bow and every tongue shall confess that He is Lord to the glory of God. He promised that if you are born again, you will see and enter the Kingdom. He will give you a new foundation as a citizen of the Kingdom of God. The King has an appointment of service for you in the embassy.

Our King is coming back and He will judge both the living and the dead. Right now, He's our King, sitting on the throne, but the Bible says one day He will be our Judge. So you want to make sure that your works survive the judgment on that Day. Our King has made a way out of no way so that we could be reconciled with the Father. Therefore, our connection to the Creator God must be a relationship, not religion. *Our King is the King of the Kingdom, not a King of the church.* Churches from every part of the world have picked up and are picking up the keys to the Kingdom, representing all kinds of ethnic persuasions. Now the family of God, they are your 'blood' brothers and sisters, and they are actively presenting the gospel of the Kingdom to the elect worldwide and opening the gates of the Kingdom with their keys — expanding the Kingdom for His glory. The question is: are you a part of this church or are you still participating in Laodicea? Jesus said learn of Him, learn of His Kingdom; your keys are waiting for you!

THE OVERCOMING REMNANT

Well, beloved, we are in a prophetic transition and God is preparing to use His remnant. The remnant represents believers that hear Jesus knocking, open the doors and come out to dine with Him. In the Greek, Christ's knock on the doors of the Laodicean church is in the present tense, which means He *continues to knock* (Revelation 3:20). Christ is still seeking to save those who are trapped in the church. Remember, God does not sit in the church. His throne is not in a church. His throne is in the Kingdom. The church is a place of service for the *ekklesia*, those called out to be an inhabitation; the church is just a reflection of Christ's Kingdom. So if you want God, you must come into the Kingdom.

We must expand the borders of the Kingdom message! The Bible says, *"But evil men and seducers shall wax worse and worse, deceiving, and being deceived."* [2 Timothy 3:13] There is a desperate need to spread the message of the King to try and rescue as many people as possible before the Lord returns. There are folks that are going to hell because the church has lost its original mission and is controlled by Satan's emissaries: money, race, and culture. When you consider that Christ came teaching the Kingdom of God, that the 1st century Christian existed in a Kingdom context, and that Paul taught the things concerning Christ and His Kingdom, we must ask ourselves 'why are we focusing so much upon the church'. The remnant realizes that they are here on official business, not merely playing with toys of the flesh. The message of the church is irrelevant, but the message of the embassy, the spiritual church, the real ecclesia is *life changing*.

What is the message of the embassy church? That our King is above all other kings, hence, He is King of Kings and Lord of Lords. He is high and lifted up, and the train of His robe fills His temple. Our King is a just and merciful King. Our King and Lord authenticated His throne by His death, burial, and resurrection. Our King is the redeeming King. Our King has power over life and death. Our King is a God of a second chance. Elijah felt overwhelmed after his encounter with Jezebel and thought he was the only true prophet around. Then, God summoned 7,000 prophets who had not bowed their knee to Baal (1 Kings 19:18). It may not seem like it but God has thousands of men and women that have not compromised and bowed their knees to Laodicea. God has a people on the back side of the mountain that He has preserved for such a time as this. There are five fold ministry gifts and lay leaders that God has in storage and is about to take them off of the shelf and put them on the floor.

You may be reading this book and it is registering with your spirit. You have often times felt like giving up because, though you know the Word God put in your mouth is an accurate word, people have ignored it. Well, it is no accident that you are reading this book; this book is a God-appointed reading for you. You may have never in your life heard of Dr. Dana Carson but something led you to this book. I believe that God led you to this book so that either you would come out of Laodicea or be encouraged to continue your Great Commission-based ministry because your time is around the corner. Your greatest hour is about to begin, so do not be weary in your race because there are multitudes depending on you! God is about to raise up people that no one knows; they may not be seen on TBN, Word Network, Daystar, or the Church Channel, but they have been faithful in persevering to win souls for God. Just like the scripture provides a picture of the closed doors of the Laodicean church, the scriptures also provide a prophetic picture of the remnant church.

It is my strong contention that revival is on the way. This revival is not going to turn Laodicea around - that is a fixed prophecy - but it will bring in a new harvest — a harvest that is fresh and focused on the things of God, not the things of this world. I believe that the Bible teaches us through the Jewish feasts and the prophetic utterances of Joel and Peter that the Kingdom church will be partakers of one of the greatest revivals in history. This revival will be marked with miracles and spiritual authority that casts out demons, heals the sick, and sets the captives free! This hope is rooted in the three journeys of Israel listed in Leviticus 23. First Corinthians 15:46 teaches the principle of first the natural and then the spiritual; first, the Old Testament then the New Testament; first, the law, then grace! The Old Testament is the New Testament concealed and the New Testament is the Old Testament revealed. The preaching of the New Testament church was preached from the Hebrew Scriptures or what we call the Old Testament. Taking this into account, the feasts of Israel represent the holistic experience of God's people in three journeys or encounters with God (Deuteronomy 16:16).

The first journey is summed up in the feast of Unleavened Bread, Passover, and First fruits. These three feasts speak of that which would happen concerning salvation. Salvation would have nothing to do with flesh or works, and it would be offered through someone who was sinless (unleavened). This salvation would be secured by the blood of Christ

(Passover). Then Christ would be the first to rise from the dead and die no more (First Fruits). The second journey was the Feast of Weeks or Pentecost. This feast spoke of the Day of Pentecost (Acts 2:1). The third journey consisted of the Feast of Trumpets, Day of Atonement, and the Feast of Tabernacles. This feast reflects the eschatological aspect of the covenant community of God. These three experiences are to be experienced by every believer. The first is salvation by the resurrected Savior who died on a cross and shed His blood but rose on the third day. The second experience is the empowerment for service through the gift of the Holy Spirit accompanied by a special prayer language. The last and third experience is the rapture of the Kingdom-minded church and the Laodicean church that remains. What does all of this have to do with the doors of the church being closed, the issuance of the keys to the Kingdom and revival?

Israel's experience with these feasts is connected to two major crop harvests: one in the spring and one in the fall. Prior to the harvest, they would have a rain that would provide what was needed for the harvest. The two rainy seasons of Israel are called the former rain and the latter rain. Remember these rains were given to ensure the harvest; without rain, there is no harvest. The former rain is associated with the second journey (Pentecost) and the latter rain is associated with the third journey. The first journey refers to the blood of the Passover and 50 days later, the children of Israel would bring in the initial harvest, resulting from the former rain. The day of Pentecost represents the initial harvest; however, there still remains the Feast of Tabernacles. Acts 2 clearly states that the day of Pentecost was the ultimate fulfillment of the second journey and fourth feast that was celebrated alone. Joel 2:28 prophesied this experience and said that it shall come to pass. Peter quotes Joel as he answers the question of what is happening by saying "this is that which the prophet Joel spoke of........" Peter, however, replaces a time term, 'afterwards' within the latter day (Acts 2:17). In doing so, Peter positions the people of God for the Feast of Tabernacles or the latter rain.

Before the Rapture of the church, there will be a great revival before another tremendous harvest represented by the Feast of Tabernacles (Leviticus 23:33-43). Tabernacles was the feast where Israel would bring in the last annual harvest, place it in baskets, take it to their roof tops and remain there for seven days, thanking God for the harvest! While the tribulation period or Daniel's 70th week is taking place on earth, a banquet will be taking place in heaven with the Kingdom-minded church (1 Thessalonians 4:16-18). Dr Carson, is this biblically based? In the Bible, Daniel's 70th week is recorded in Daniel 9:25-27, according to eschatologist Hal Lindsey. The final seven years or Daniel's 70th week begins with the signing of a protective treaty between Israel and the Anti-Christ, who will come from the revived Roman Empire, comprised of the 10 European nations (Daniel 9:27). This period begins the Tribulation period and right before the Rapture or the great snatch. This understanding is based upon the following: Daniel's writing states that 69 weeks of years (483 years) would pass and the Messiah would be cut off (Daniel 9:25-26). Then, the last week of years, which total 490 years, would be completed. These years denote years of exile and punishment that were exclusively assigned to Israel and then the 70th week culminates in the Tribulation period. While there are several Tribulation options among church scholars, I believe that the scriptures teach a pre-Tribulation paradigm. However, there are those who are mid-Tribulationists and post-Tribulationists; they believe that the Rapture will take place in the middle of Daniel's 70th week and at the end of the 70th week, respectively. But before the Rapture of the church takes place, there will be a revival! While I would love to further discuss the Rapture and the church, that is another book but please visit my website for additional information concerning the Book of Revelation.

Who will be conducting this revival? And who will God use for His final campaign to announce the time is now? In the book of Revelation, only the Kingdom-minded church is promised that she will be kept from the hour of trial. It will not be Laodicea, who is preoccupied with earnings or "faith for increase". Nor will it be those who are trying to preserve the purity of their race by any means necessary. The revival will be conducted by those who are willing to take advantage of the open door to preach the gospel of the Kingdom of God. This last dispensation of the theological renewal will experience a tremendous revival. I believe that this revival will touch the hearts of young people who will come to God in Kingdom power. This revival will be the last showdown between Satan and the true church. The key of David will unlock the secret to the hearts of young people who the church has lost favor with. The key of David will create an opening for global missions. The key of David will allow those who desire to preach the gospel world wide to do so.

"But what about the church of Laodicea?" They will be busy doing what they do naturally — cutting deals, making money, and preserving their superiority. Meanwhile, the Kingdom-minded church will be making disciples that function as Kingdom citizens that are no longer hung up on race, class, and sex. How will this movement be seen? Quite honestly, the world will see their actions as an extremist movement and the Laodicean Church will be the most inflamed about what God is doing. The Laodicean church will continue to gain greater popularity among the world and sinners because of its message of inspiration and motivation, void of transformation by the Spirit of God. The Laodicean message makes everyone feel good because the pulpit is mounted weekly by encouragers, motivators, and exhorters, but not gospel preachers that have sermons rooted in the scriptures. The church of Laodicea doesn't need the anointing nor does it need the power of God, for it has the power of seduction and allurement that causes one to *feel* 'at-one-ment' with God. The message of Laodicea will have two ultimate focuses: 1) Life on earth can be lived to its fullest through the accumulation of wealth, and 2) conform to our cultural norms because our norms are God's norms. Why? Because the doors of the church are closed!

My prayer is that you seriously pray about the things discussed in this book and that you respond to what the Spirit of God communicates to you. If you are a leader in a Laodicean church, pray about God helping you re-position the church into a Kingdom church or pray about removing yourself. If you are a member of a Laodicean church, listen to the voice of Jesus and invite Him in to dine with you in His Word. Come out of Laodicea! If you are a leader in a transition church, lead your church in a Kingdom transition as God educates you in the Kingdom. If you are involved in a transition church, pray for your leadership that God would give them a Kingdom coach or mentor who will be able to assist the church in their transition. But remember — HEAR HIS VOICE! Let He that have an ear, hear what the Spirit is saying to the churches!

ENDNOTES PAGE

1. Mostyn, Carolynn. *"Who are Local Churches Building for?"* Connection: Good News Magazine. February 16, 2005. <http://www.connectionmagazine.org>
2. <http://www.reuters.com/article/lifestyleMolt/idUSN2521944020080225>. "Many Americans Religiously Unaffiliated: Survey"
3. <http://pewforum.org/>. January 2008. Pew Forum on Religion and Public Life: U.S. Religious Landscape Survey. Retrieved March 3, 2008.
4. Fuellenbach, John. *The Kingdom of God: The Message of Jesus Today*. Maryknoll: Orbis Books, 1995. p. 243
5. Ladd, George Eldon. *Gospel of the Kingdom: Scriptural Studies in the Kingdom of God*. Grand Rapids: Eerdmans Publishing Company, 1959.
6. Fuellenbach, John. The Kingdom of God : The Message of Jesus Today. Maryknoll: Orbis Books, 1995.
7. González, Justo L. *The Early Church to the Dawn of the Reformation*. San Francisco: Harper & Row Publishers, 1985.
8. Fuller Theological Seminary Study

9. <http://pewforum.org/>. January 2008. Pew Forum on Religion and Public Life: U.S. Religious Landscape Survey. Retrieved March 3, 2008.

10. González, Justo L. *The Early Church to the Dawn of the Reformation*. San Francisco: Harper & Row Publishers, 1985.

11. Yancey, Philip. *What's So Amazing About Grace?* Grand Rapids: Zondervan, 2002.

12. Carroll, Charles. *A Negro, A Beast or in the Image of God?* St. Louis: American Book and Bible House, 1900.

13. Frazier, E. Franklin and C.E. Lincoln. *The Negro Church in America/The Black Church Since Frazier*. New York: Schocken Books, 1974.

14. Emerson, Michael O. and Christian Smith. *Divided by Faith: Evangelical Religion and the Problem of Race in America*. New York: Oxford University Press, 2001.

15. Luther, Dr. Martin, *"Disputation of Dr. Martin Luther on the Power and the Efficacy of Indulgences* (1517)." Works of Martin Luther: Adolph Spaeth, L.D. Reed, Henry Eyster Jacobs, et Al., Trans. & Eds. (Philadelphia: A. J. Holman Company, 1915), Vol.1, pp. 29-38

16. Luther, Martin and Stephen J. Nicols, *Martin Luther's 95 Theses*. Phillipsburg: P & R Publishing, 2003

17. Niebuhr, Richard H. *Christ and Culture*. New York : Harper & Row Publishers, 1951

18. Vlach, Michael J. "Crisis in America 's Churches: Bible Knowledge at All-Time Low." Theological Studies. 26 February 2008. <http://www.theologicalstudies.citymax.com> Retrieved March 3, 2008

19. Niebuhr, H. Richard. *The Kingdom of God in America*. Middleton: Wesleyan, 1988.

20. Bonhoeffer, Dietrich. *The Cost of Discipleship*. New York : MacMillan, 1959.

BIBLIOGRAPHY AND SUGGESTED READINGS

Beasley-Murray, G.R. *Jesus and the Kingdom of God*. Grand Rapids: Eerdmans, 1986.

Bercot, David W.(ed). *A Dictionary of Early Christian Beliefs: A Reference Guide to More than 700 Topics Discussed by the Early Church Fathers*. Peabody: Hendrickson, 1998.

Bourke, Vernon J. *Saint Augustine: City of God*. New York: Doubleday, 1958.

Bright, John. *The Kingdom of God: The Biblical Concept and Its Meaning for the Church*.
Nashville, Abingdon Press, 1981.

Burtner Robert W. And Robert E. Chiles (eds). *John Wesley's Theology: A Collection from His Works*. Nashville: Abingdon Press, 1982.

Carroll, Charles. *A Negro, A Beast or in the Image of God?* St. Louis: American Book and Bible House, 1900.

DeYoung, Curtiss Paul, Michael Emerson, George Yancy, and Karen Chai Kim. *United By Faith: The Multiracial Congregation as an Answer to the Problem of Race*. New York: Oxford University Press, 2003.

Erickson, Millard J. *Christian Theology*. Grand Rapids: Baker Books, 1998.

Emerson, Michael O. and Christian Smith. *Divided by Faith*. New York: Oxford University Press, 2001.

Fuellenbach, John. *The Kingdom of God: The Message of Jesus Today*. Maryknoll: Orbis Books, 1995.

Frazier, E. Franklin and C.E. Lincoln. *The Negro Church in America/The Black Church Since Frazier*. New York: Schocken Books, 1974.

González, Justo L. *The Early Church to the Dawn of the Reformation*. San Francisco: Harper & Row Publishers, 1985.

González, Justo L. *The Story of Christianity: The Reformation to the Present Day*. San Francisco: Harper & Row Publishers, 1985.

Kistler, Don(ed). *Pressing into the Kingdom: Jonathan Edwards on Seeking Salvation*. Morgan: Soli Deo Gloria Publications, 1998.

Kurian, George Thomas (ed). *Nelson's Dictionary of Christianity: The Authoritative Resource on the Christian World*. Nashville: Thomas Nelson, 2005.

LaHaye, Tim. *Revelation: Illustrated and Made Plain*. Grand Rapids: Lamplighter Books, 1975.

Lloyd-Jones, Martyn. *The Kingdom of God*. Langley: Crossway, 1992.

Lovett, Leonard. *Kingdom Beyond Color: Re-examining the Phenomenon of Racism*. Philadelphia: Xlibris, 2006.

Moore, Russell D. *The Kingdom of Christ: The New Evangelical Perspective*. Wheaton: Crossway, 2004.

Niebuhr, H. Richard. *The Kingdom of God in America*. Middleton: Wesleyan, 1988.

Raboteau, Albert. *A Fire in the Bones: Reflections on African American Religious History*. Boston: Beacon Press, 1995.

Rabateau, Albert J. *Slave Religion: The "Invisible Institution" in the Antebellum South.* New York: Oxford University Press, 1978.

Torbett, David. *Theology and Slavery: Charles Hodge and Horace Bushnell.* Mercer University Press, 2006.

Walsh, Gerald G., Demetrius B. Zema, Grace Monahan, and Daniel Honan.

Wesley, John. *The Nature of the Kingdom.* Minneapolis: Bethany House Publishers, 1979.

Yancey, Philip. *What's So Amazing About Grace?* Grand Rapids: Zondervan, 2002.

Coming soon! Lord, Help, I'm Trapped in the Church!

Stay on the lookout for the next book in this revolutionary series on the state of Christian Church. This book will inform you about the things that are happening behind the doors of the church that Jesus is knocking on in Revelation 3:20. "Lord Help" outlines the traps that have people bound and afraid to come out of traditionalism. This book will teach you how church loyalty can send you to a condemnatory future. This book also provides for pastors, laymen, and churches, some strategies for taking your ministry from a Laodicean Model to a Kingdom Model church. Discover ways to escape from social bondage into spiritual freedom. And receive emancipation for your soul!

Coming soon! "The Kingdom not the Church: How to Ensure that You are a Part of God's End Time Reformation & Revival!

This book will help you to understand the relevance of the church in its relationship to the Kingdom of God. Learn what Christ, the disciples, and the early church emphasized

— The Kingdom. By reading this book, you will grasp and understand the mandate of the Kingdom and how the sociological church has placed Christ on the outside and maneuvered a hostile take over. Receive a sound biblical and theological understanding of the Kingdom of God and what it means to allow God to reign as King in your life. This book is not a fad; it is the revelation of God made plain concerning His Kingdom and His church!

For more Kingdom resources, visit online at TheKingdomSuperstore.com:
Your #1 resource for information on the Kingdom of God or visit the website at: www.danacarsonministries. com

Kingdom instruction is available for you! Dr. Dana Carson invites you to enroll in the Carson Kingdom Institute of Ministerial and Theological Studies (CKI). CKI trains Kingdom leaders for their God-given purpose by providing a practical, relevant, and Biblically sound education that will enable leaders to boldly impact the world with the power of gospel of Jesus Christ. **The Kingdom of God Leadership program** specifically assists leaders in understanding the Kingdom of God as prophesied in the Old Testament, proclaimed and explained in the Gospels, perpetuated in the New Testament church, and fully realized in this dispensation. Register today to become a 21st century Kingdom Leader at www.danacarsonministries.com/CKI!